TENDERLOIN

TENDERLOIN

A New Musical Comedy

(Based on the novel by Samuel Hopkins Adams)

Book by JEROME WEIDMAN *and* GEORGE ABBOTT

Music by JERRY BOCK

Lyrics by SHELDON HARNICK

 Random House, New York

Photographs by courtesy of Eileen Darby-Graphic House

Manufactured in the United States of America

TENDERLOIN *was first presented by Robert E. Griffith and Harold S. Prince at the Forty-sixth Street Theatre on October 17, 1960, with the following cast:*

(In order of appearance)

TOMMY	Ron Husmann
NITA	Eileen Rodgers
LT. SCHMIDT (THE PANTATA)	Ralph Dunn
REVEREND BROCK	Maurice Evans
GERTIE	Lee Becker
MARGIE	Margery Gray
GIRL	Dorothy Frank
GIRL	Patsy Peterson
YOUNG MAN	Dargan Montgomery
JESSICA	Irene Kane
LAURA	Wynne Miller
ELLINGTON	Gordon Cook
PURDY	Raymond Bramley
JOE	Rex Everhart
MARTIN	Lanier Davis
DEACON	Roy Fant
ROONEY	Jordon Howard
NELLIE	Marguerite Shaw
SERGEANT	Michael Roberts
COP	Jack McCann
FRYE	Eddie Phillips
PROSTITUTES	Erin Martin, Margery Gray
DRUNK	Bob Fitch
MAGGIE	Pat Turner
LIZ	Christine Norden
MRS. BARKER	Elaine Rogers
CHAIRMAN	Joe Hill

DANCERS: Jere Admire, David Evans, Bob Fitch, Dorothy Frank, Margery Gray, Mickey Gunnersen, Sandy Leeds, Jack Leigh, Erin Martin, Marjorie Pragon, Wakefield Poole, Ron Stratton, Jayne Turner, Pat Turner.

SINGERS: Charles Aschmann, Carvel Carter, Nancy Emes, John Ford, Stokeley Gray, Maria Graziano, Joe Hill, Jordon Howard, Gail Johnston, Jack McCann, Dargan Montgomery, Patsy Peterson, Claire Richard, Michael Roberts, Elaine Rogers

Production directed by George Abbott
Sets and costumes by Cecil Beaton
Dances and musical numbers staged by Joe Layton
Musical direction by Hal Hastings
Orchestrations by Irwin Kostal
Dance music arranged by Jack Elliott

The action takes place on the Island of Manhattan in the latter part of the nineteenth century.

There are two acts.

MUSICAL NUMBERS

ACT ONE

"Bless This Land" — THE CHOIR
"Little Old New York"
> EILEEN RODGERS, LEE BECKER and COMPANY

"Dr. Brock" — MAURICE EVANS
"Artificial Flowers" — RON HUSMANN
"What's in It for You?"
> MAURICE EVANS and RON HUSMANN

"Reform" — LEE BECKER, NANCY EMES, CARVEL CARTER
"Tommy, Tommy" — WYNNE MILLER
"Artificial Flowers" Reprise — MARGERY GRAY
"The Picture of Happiness" — RON HUSMANN
"Dance" — LEE BECKER, EDDIE PHILLIPS and COMPANY
"Dear Friend" — MAURICE EVANS, WYNNE MILLER,
> IRENE KANE, JAYNE TURNER

"The Army of the Just" — MAURICE EVANS, LANIER DAVIS,
> JACK LEIGH, CHARLES ASCHMANN, STOKELEY GRAY

"How the Money Changes Hands"
> MAURICE EVANS, EILEEN RODGERS, CHRISTINE NORDEN,
> EDDIE PHILLIPS, LEE BECKER and COMPANY

ACT TWO

"Good Clean Fun" — MAURICE EVANS and COMPANY
"My Miss Mary" — RON HUSMANN, WYNNE MILLER
> and SINGERS

"My Gentle Young Johnny" — EILEEN RODGERS
"The Trial" — COMPANY
"The Tenderloin Celebration" — EDDIE PHILLIPS, LEE BECKER
> and COMPANY

"Reform" Reprise — LEE BECKER, MARGERY GRAY,
> CHRISTINE NORDEN and COMPANY

"Tommy, Tommy" Reprise — WYNNE MILLER
"Little Old New York" Reprise — COMPANY

ACT ONE

Scene 1

At rise, the stage is dark.

Music.

The lights pick up TOMMY *at left. His clothes are turn-of-the-century, cheap and flashy.*

He speaks from Limbo.

TOMMY   You heard of Horatio Alger? That's gonna be me. Right to the top, and I don't care how. Nuttin' can stop me— I mean nothing. See? I'm improvin' already. Listen! I got a crummy job as a reporter on the *Tatler* magazine; and down in that joint in the Tenderloin, what am I? Just a four-bit singer. But you watch where I go. Cause this is the land of opportunity.

> (*Music. The light fades on* TOMMY *and picks up* NITA *at left center. She wears the gaudy costume of a successful prostitute*)

NITA (*She speaks from Limbo*)   When I was a kid, we didn't have hardly enough to eat. Then we come to this country and I find out I have something men will pay for. I'm now the highest-priced girl in the Tenderloin. For America is indeed the land of opportunity.

> (*Music. The light fades on* NITA *and picks up* SCHMIDT *at center. He wears the uniform of a police lieutenant*)

3

SCHMIDT (*He speaks from Limbo*) I have just been assigned
to the Nineteenth Precinct—the Tenderloin. And there I
get my percentage off of everybody and everything. In five
years, I'll be rich. For this here is sure the land of opportunity.

> (*Music. The light fades on* SCHMIDT *and picks up the
> choir, right*)

CHOIR (*Singing*)
> Bless this land of freedom and friendship
> Bless this land of hope and of promise
> Land that offers faith in the future
> Help to the fallen
> Home to the homeless
> Bless this land of gleaming abundance
> Land where we can say to our children
> Here you need not bow to your betters
> Here you are equal
> Here you may proudly stand
> (Opportunity for all)
> Bless this golden land.

> (REVEREND BROCK *mounts the pulpit at right and the
> choir exits at right.* BROCK *wears a Prince Albert coat
> and a beard*)

BROCK (*On pulpit at right*) There have been certain gentlemen of the press who have considered my words on the
subject of the Tenderloin to be shocking. Good. I want them
to be shocking. Because I am speaking of a shocking thing.
I am speaking of a district so lawless, so immoral, as to be
in truth a present-day Sodom and Gomorrah. This district
is not in Shanghai, not in far-off Bombay. No, my friends,
it stands at your very door. From Fourteenth to Forty-second

4

Street, from Fourth Avenue to the Hudson, this monument to harlotry stands mocking us. Here crime flourishes. Here debaucheries of every type are for sale nightly, including Sunday. Shall we look the other way? While corrupt politicians and our police force condone this situation? No, no, no, my friends. I ask for your good will, your courage, your influence. I ask each and every one of you to join me in a great crusade against this noisome pestilence. People of New York City, we must close the Tenderloin.

(*The light fades on him.* NITA *is seen alone on the vast emptiness of the stage in a single light*)

NITA Mind your own business. Tend to your church. Leave us alone.

(*The light picks up* SCHMIDT *and three cops at right*)

SCHMIDT We got prosperity. We got good times. Keep your nose out of it.

(GERTIE *appears beside* NITA)

GERTIE Is that a Christian thing to do? Put everybody out of work?

MARGIE (*Appearing out of the darkness*) What do you want to come buttin' in on us for?

GIRL (*Disgusted*) Some people always want to change everything.

NITA Why don't you mind your own business?

MARGIE Everybody's happy.

NITA New York's the biggest city, ain't it?

5

GERTIE Yeah, if you had any sense, you'd leave it alone. (*Music*) That'd be my advice, leave it the way it is.

NITA (*Singing*)
Why can't this damn do-gooder
Keep his hands off
Little . . . Old New . . .

GERTIE
Little Old New York
Is plenty good enough for me

NITA
Good enough for me

BOTH
Good enough for me

NITA, GERTIE, MARGIE *and* GIRL
Little Old New York
Is plenty good enough for me

GIRLS *and* COPS
Keep your hands off Little Old New York.

NITA
Don't want no bible spoutin'

GERTIE
Gospel shoutin'

BOTH
Preacher nosin' aroun'
Dryin' everythin' up

6

Closin' everythin' down
Don't want no roly-poly, holy-boly
Purifyin' the town
Not my Little Old New York.

Right now she's wide open
Here's hopin'
She'll always be this way
Right now she's wide open
Anyone doesn't like it here
He don't have to stay.

Little Old New York
Is plenty good enough for me
Good enough for me
Good enough for me
Little Old New York
Is plenty good enough for me.

NITA

Lots of pork

GERTIE

In Little Old New York.

NITA

We got a golden goose here

GERTIE

Runnin' loose here

BOTH

We don't need to compete

TENDERLOIN

Let the minister work
The other side of the street
That way we're all in clover
With enough left over
To tip the cop on the beat
That's my Little Old New York.

This town has four millions
And more millions
Are headin' right this way
This town has four millions
There are millions to be made
It's happ'nin' every day.

(During number, stage fills up with Tenderloin characters: drunks, swells, the madam, pickpockets, etc.)

Little Old New York
Is plenty good enough for me
Good enough for me
Good enough for me
Little Old New York
Is plenty good enough for me
Keep your hands off
Little Old New York.

Little Old New York
Is plenty good enough for me
Big enough for me
Rich enough for me
Little Old New York
Is plenty good enough for me

Listen preacher
Keep your hands off
Little . . . Old New . . .

NITA *and* GERTIE

Yo . . .

GIRLS

Little Old New York
Is plenty good enough
for me
Little Old New York

ALL

Little N. Y. C. Yeah!

Blackout

ship

SCENE 2

A street outside the church.

At rise, two parishioners are standing in front of the Parish House door. Others cross slowly downstage. All are dressed in fashionable 1890's costumes.

YOUNG MAN That's the best thing about this church. The social events.

GIRL Yes, and we always have good weather.

YOUNG MAN Maybe Dr. Brock puts in a good word with . . . (*He points up*) you know . . .
    (TOMMY *comes out of the Parish House*)

GIRL (*To* YOUNG MAN) Oh, Richard . . . don't be sacrilegious.
    (JESSICA *comes out of the Parish House with a cane*)

JESSICA Oh, mister! (TOMMY *turns*) You forgot your cane.
    (*She moves to right center as the group exits through the door into the Parish House*)

TOMMY Look, you're a sweet girl, can't you at least ask him?

JESSICA Dr. Brock gave orders . . . I wouldn't dare . . . but you can come back with the other reporters, this afternoon.

TOMMY I don't stand a chance with those other reporters from the dailies. I gotta get there first.

JESSICA But is that ethical?

TOMMY I don't want to be ethical. I want to get a scoop. If John D. Rockefeller finds an oil well, does he go around and tell Jay Gould where it is?

LAURA (*Offstage at left*) Yoohoo!

JESSICA (*Crossing at center toward left*) Yoohoo! Oh, hello. (*To* TOMMY) Isn't she beautiful?

TOMMY (*Looking off left*) Sure, she looks kind of familiar. She looks like, you know, that society girl in the papers . . . that Laura Crosbie.

JESSICA It *is* Laura Crosbie.

TOMMY It is? What's she doing here? Hey, gimme my cane. (*He snatches his cane and strikes a fraudulently elegant pose.* LAURA *and* ELLINGTON *enter downstage at left.* LAURA *crosses to* JESSICA)

LAURA You've got a new suit, Jessica. You look lovely. May I present Ellington Dupont Smythe the Second . . . Ellington, this is my friend, Jessica Havemeyer.

ELLINGTON How do you do?

JESSICA (*Flustered*) I'm pleased to meet you.

LAURA Jessica is the boss of the Parish House.

JESSICA (*Protesting awkwardly*) Oh, I just do some work here
. . . I'm not . . . (*She crosses toward right*) Laura, your
uncle's inside talking to that Mr. Kovack. (*At door of Parish
House*) I'm not really the boss at all.
(*She exits into the Parish House*)

ELLINGTON Is that why you sing in the choir? On account of
your uncle?

LAURA (*Crossing to door of Parish House*) No, because I
like it.

ELLINGTON But it takes you away so much.

LAURA (*Smiling*) Why don't *you* join? You have a lovely
voice. Good-bye.
(*She exits.* ELLINGTON *shrugs, turns, jauntily twirls his
cane and exits downstage at left*)

TOMMY (*Looking after* ELLINGTON *and twirling his cane in
imitation of the elegant young swell*) The Second, huh?
(*Gets an idea, knocks on the door of the Parish House.*
JESSICA *answers and* TOMMY *pulls* JESSICA *out of the door-
way*)

JESSICA (*Protesting*) Please, I told you, I can't—

TOMMY No, come out here for a minute.

JESSICA What is it?

TOMMY I was just joking with you, miss, about that interview. I couldn't get up the courage to tell you what I really
want.

JESSICA Yes?

TOMMY (*Soulful*) I'd like to join the choir.

Blackout

Scene 3

Parish House.

At rise, PURDY *is discovered at right of center and* JOE KOVACK *at left of center.* PURDY *is an elderly, prosperous, well-dressed businessman.* JOE *is a country yokel.*

PURDY (*Firm*) Kovack, it's our duty to let Dr. Brock know how some of his parishioners feel.

JOE (*Uneasy*) I don't like to argue with the Reverend Brock. After all, he's closer to God than I am.

PURDY You're close enough for practical purposes. And you're a good man.

JOE I don't know if I'm good. I been having the most sinful dreams lately. (BROCK *enters from office and crosses to left of* JOE) Ever since I got rich, I keep thinking of temptation.

BROCK (*Laughs*) Joe, if all my sinners were as wicked as you, I'd be out of a job.

PURDY Dr. Brock, we've got to talk to you.

BROCK Well, Brother Purdy, and what's the crisis today?

PURDY Your last Sunday's sermon. And it may interest you to know that Brother Kovack here agrees with me.

BROCK Do you, Joe?

JOE Well—well, some of the people down my way—they think it's a scandal to have a minister saying such bad things right out there in public. Now, I'm with you Dr. Brock, and I'd follow you straight to hell.

BROCK I trust that won't be necessary.

PURDY Dr. Brock, there are times when we must be tolerant —must be practical about the ways of the world.

BROCK Tolerant I believe I am. Tolerant of sinners. But I do not think God meant us to be tolerant of sin. Brother Purdy, I see my duty clearly, so very clearly.
      (MARTIN, *the choirmaster, enters at right*)

MARTIN Dr. Brock?

BROCK (*To* PURDY *and* JOE) Go into my office, both of you, and read some of the mail I've received on the subject.

MARTIN It's about your lecture to the Ladies Auxiliary—?

BROCK (*To* PURDY *and* JOE) The letters in the little pile are the ones that disapprove of what I'm doing.
      (PURDY *and* JOE *exit through the upstage door*)

MARTIN The ladies suggested that instead of your subject being local slum conditions, you give them your talk about the Holy Land.

BROCK (*Sighs wearily*) Very well.

TENDERLOIN

MARTIN (*Exiting downstage at right*)   Thank you, Dr. Brock.
   (*music*)

BROCK (*Singing*)
   Dr. Brock, close your eyes
   You should not be worldly-wise
   Speak to us of lofty things
   First Corinthians, Second Kings
   Dr. Brock, do everything in your power
   To keep our church a glorious ivory tower.

   If I prepared the sort of simple sermon
   That some of my parishioners expect
   I might as well be speaking French or German
   I'd get the same effect.

   I know the kind of sermon that's in fashion
   But that's the kind of drivel I deplore
   Denounce the sins of Babylon with passion
   But skip the sins next door.

   Dr. Brock, we beseech
   Please be careful what you preach
   Speak of Jericho, speak of Job
   Speak of Joseph's colorful robe
   Leave us with a beautiful phrase on Sunday
   But let us go our separate ways on Monday.

   They say to me with patronizing unction
   Confine yourself to biblical research
   They seem to feel religion has a function
   But not outside the church.

They love to hear the music of the organ
They love to hear the voices of the choir
When all the while it's really J. P. Morgan
Who sets them on fire!
Andrew Brock, be yourself
Andrew Brock, you must speak
Every day of the week!
> (BROCK *exits through upstage door.* JESSICA *enters upstage at left with* TOMMY. LAURA *and* CHOIR GIRLS *follow*)

JESSICA (*To* TOMMY) You wait right there. I'll call Mr. Martin. (*She exits downstage at right*)

TOMMY Miss Crosbie?

LAURA (*Stops and turns*) Yes?

TOMMY Miss Crosbie—(*Moves a few steps*)—will you excuse the intrusion? But could you tell me is the Reverend Andrew Brock in that room? (*Points toward office*) Is that his office?

LAURA Yes, I believe so.

TOMMY I'd like to get a chance to speak to him. Do you think it could be arranged that I have a word with him?

LAURA I'm not the one to ask. I—

TOMMY Permit me to introduce myself. I'm Thomas Howatt the Second. I mean I know you're a society girl. I've heard some nice things about you from some of the other society people who I'm intimate friends with. It ain't exactly New

York where I come from, but we have our own Four Hundred—and of course, my dad was the Mayor.

LAURA (*Dry*) Congratulations!

TOMMY And I know you must be in good with the Reverend. I mean you must be a favorite on account of your uncle and, you know, so if you was to speak to him regarding he give me an interview, it certainly would be appreciated by my many society friends and I also.

LAURA You exaggerate my influence, Mr.— Mr.—?

TOMMY Thomas Howatt—(*Pause*)—the Second.
(JESSICA *enters downstage right and crosses upstage left in front of* LAURA)

JESSICA (*To* TOMMY) Mr. Martin will be right out.

LAURA (*To* TOMMY) I'm sorry I can't be of more help.

TOMMY I'll be around. We'll talk it over.
(LAURA *exits downstage at right as* MARTIN *enters downstage at right*)

MARTIN (*To* JESSICA) Is this the gentleman?

JESSICA Yes, sir.

MARTIN (*To* TOMMY) Do you wish to speak to me?

TOMMY Are you the guy—the one who's in charge of the choir?

MARTIN (*Cool*) I'm the choirmaster.

TOMMY I'd like to join.
    (JESSICA *exits upstage at left*)

MARTIN You have sung in choirs before?

TOMMY Well, not in choirs exactly, but I've done quite a lot
of singing in different places.

MARTIN Would you care to give one of these as a reference?

TOMMY (*Quickly*) No, no, you wouldn't know about them.

MARTIN Are you a member of this church?

TOMMY No, I'm not—but I'm in favor of it. I think I'd fit in
here pretty good.

MARTIN (*Cold*) What is your denomination?

TOMMY Huh? Oh, I'll do it for free.

MARTIN (*Icy*) My impression is that you do not belong to our
church nor to any other church. I'm sorry. We won't be able
to use you.

TOMMY Ain't you going to hear me sing?

MARTIN That won't be necessary. Good day.
    (*He goes out at right.* TOMMY *crosses to the left, discon-
    solate, then suddenly he gets an idea. He goes over,
    gently opens the door to* BROCK's *office, and sings*)

TENDERLOIN

TOMMY (*Singing*)

Alone in the world was poor little Ann
As sweet a young child as you'd find
Her parents had gone to their final reward
Leaving their darling behind
This poor little child was but nine years of age
When Mother and Dad went away
But bravely she worked at the one thing she knew
To earn her few pennies each day.

She made
Artificial flowers
Artificial flowers
Flowers for ladies of fashion to wear
Artificial flowers
Artificial flowers
Fashioned from Annie's despair.

With paper and shears, with wire and wax
She fashioned each tulip and mum
As snow drifted in to her tenement room
Her dear little fingers grew numb
With paper and shears, with wire and wax
She labored and never complained
'Til cutting and folding her health slipped away
And wiring and waxing, she waned.

(*By now*, BROCK, PURDY, JOE, LAURA, JESSICA *and members of the choir have entered to listen*)

BROCK My boy, you have a very pleasing voice.

TOMMY (*Fake shy*) Thank you. I hoped you'd feel that way.

1

BROCK Are you with the choir?

TOMMY I'd like to be.

BROCK (*To choir lady*) Angela, send for Mr. Martin. (*She goes out downstage at right*) Where did you hear that song?

TOMMY (*Thinking fast*) I learned it—from my mother.
    (MARTIN *enters downstage at right*)

BROCK Brother Martin, I want you to listen to this.

TOMMY (*Singing*)
    Making
    Artificial flowers
    Artificial flowers
    Flowers for ladies of fashion to wear

TOMMY *and* JESSICA
    Artificial flowers
    Artificial flowers
    Fashioned from Annie's despair.

TOMMY
    They found little Ann all covered with ice
    Still clutching her poor frozen shears
    Amidst all the blossoms she fashioned by hand
    And watered with all her young tears
    There must be a heav'n where Annie can play
    In heavenly gardens and bowers
    Instead of a halo she'll wear round her head
    A garland of genuine flowers.

No more
Artificial flowers
Artificial flowers
Flowers for ladies of fashion to wear.

ALL
Artificial flowers
Artificial flowers
Fashioned from Annie's despair.

BROCK Martin, I think this young man would make a fine addition to our choir.

MARTIN (*Protesting*) Dr. Brock, he isn't even a church member!

BROCK (*To* TOMMY) What's your name, young man?

TOMMY Thomas Howatt.

BROCK I see.

TOMMY The Second.

BROCK (*Turns to the choirmaster*) Martin, you continue with the rehearsal. I'll have a little talk with Thomas. (MARTIN, *his singers and* JESSICA *and* LAURA *go out at right*) Now, young man, why do you wish to become a member of our choir?

TOMMY I heard your sermon last week and it was sort of like an inspiration, and I thought if I could get in the choir, then I might be able to meet you and I could be of some help.

BROCK Help?

TOMMY Yes, sir. I'm a newspaperman. I could wise you up on some things.

PURDY (*Disgusted*) Good grief!
      (JOE *follows* PURDY *out into the office and shuts the door*)

TOMMY (*Earnest*) You're a great orator, Dr. Brock. The greatest since Demockeles . . . I mean, Demosthenes. And maybe greater than him. But it seems like there was some things you wasn't wised up to. Now, my position as one of the ace reporters on the *Tatler* gives me a lot of info on the Tenderloin. And if I could be of any help—in fact, if you'd like me to do a little personal interview with you right now —I think most likely I could get something in print that will be a lot of assistance to you in your cause.

BROCK (*Cool*) I see. So you devote your life to good causes?

TOMMY (*Taken aback*) Well, ain't it all right? I mean, isn't it all right if I want to help?

BROCK And you are well informed concerning the Tenderloin?

TOMMY (*Hasty*) Just in the line of duty as a reporter. I'm on your side. It's a monument to harlotry and I'm against it.

BROCK Young man, why are you really here?

TOMMY I told you.

23

BROCK   I'm afraid you're a good deal of a liar.

TOMMY (*Astonished*)   Don't you trust me?

BROCK (*Turning away*)   No, my boy.

TOMMY   I'm disappointed in you—a minister not trusting people.

BROCK   You came here to get an exclusive interview . . . a scoop . . . isn't that it?

TOMMY   Well . . . (BROCK *raises a warning finger*) That's what I came for, but since I got here I feel very strong about . . . I'd like to help.

BROCK   And what do you want in return?

TOMMY (*Humble*)   Maybe you'll be a good influence on me, sir.

BROCK (*Crossing toward* TOMMY)   I see certain things in you, Thomas.

TOMMY   Where?

BROCK   Inside.

TOMMY (*Crossing away hastily to right*)   Listen, if you don't mind . . . quit lookin' in there. (*He turns*) And as far as that goes, I can look, too, you know. (*He points at* BROCK) Even Demosthenes ain't *invisible*. (*Chord. He sings*)

24

I never met no one like you
But are you what you seem?
Or does your big crusade
Hide some private scheme?

I never met no one yet
Who wasn't lookin' for his cut
You gotta be after somethin'
But I can't imagine what. . . .

What's in it for you?
What's in it for you?
What is it you're after?
I wish I knew,
I wish I knew.

BROCK (*Amused*)   And what do you see?

TOMMY   Well, I see . . . what do they call it when a fellow
thinks he's always right?

BROCK   A bigot?

TOMMY   Oh, no! I wouldn't let nobody say that about you.

BROCK   Pompous, maybe?

TOMMY   Yeah, more like that. Sort of stuffy.

BROCK (*Laughs*)   I see. Well, Thomas, I come by it naturally.
The Dutch and the Scotch are the stuffiest people in the
world, and I come from both of them. Maybe we could
learn something from each other. (*Singing*)

I certainly need assistance
But will I find it here?
There's more to you my lad
Than meets the eye or ear.

The story you tell with such aplomb
I somehow can't believe
I'm curious as to just exactly
What is up your sleeve.

BROCK	TOMMY
What's in it for you?	What's in it for you?
What's in it for you?	What's in it for you?
What is it you're after?	What is it you're after?
I wish I knew.	I wish I knew.

BROCK   Thomas, I admire ambition . . .

TOMMY   So do I.

BROCK   This afternoon at three o'clock, right after my meeting with the Mission Society, I'm going to see the police officer in charge of the Tenderloin.

TOMMY   (*Astonished*)   Personally?

BROCK   Yes.

TOMMY   Geez!

BROCK   (*Pained*)   Try to enlarge your vocabulary, Thomas. There are more educated ways of expressing surprise.

TOMMY   I got some terrible habits, Reverend, I know that.

26

BROCK   Now, it occurs to me that if you could arrange to have
a photographer there to take a picture of me coming out
of the Nineteenth Precinct Police Station, it might be something that could help you with your employer. . . .

BROCK *(Singing)*
    Shall I accept him as an
      ally?
    Maybe I'm acting like
      a fool.

    We shall see what we
      shall see
    What we shall see
    What we shall see
    What's in it for you
    My charming young
      man?
    What is it you're after?

TOMMY *(Singing)*
    I need him and
    He needs me.
    The Tenderloin ain't no
    Sunday School.

    We shall see what we
      shall see
    We shall see what we
      shall see
    We shall see what we
      shall see
    What's in it for you?
    What is it you're after?
    What plot, what plan?

BOTH
    Whatever it is that you're trying to prove

TOMMY
    You're deep

BROCK
    You're shrewd
    (They shake hands)

BOTH *(Speaking)*   Your move.

Blackout

27

SCENE 4

Street in front of the Nineteenth Precinct.

TOMMY *enters at right,* DEACON—*a seedy looking old man—following with a camera on a tripod slung over his shoulder.*

TOMMY   Now, Deacon, you get your camera set up over there and snap him when he's coming out.

DEACON   What about the money?

TOMMY   I'm paying you myself personally. The *Tatler* don't get this. I'm selling this to the dailies.

DEACON   You're pretty ambitious, aren't you?

TOMMY   You just find that out?
        (TOMMY *exits at left*)

DEACON   (*Following* TOMMY *off at left*)   No, boy. Merely an editorial comment.
        (DEACON *exits*)

Blackout

SCENE 5

The Nineteenth Precinct Police Station.

Seated and standing are prostitutes, policemen, the Dip, and a couple of drunks. NELLIE, *an older, seedier type, stands in front of the* SERGEANT's *desk, flanked by* ROONEY, *a policeman.* TOMMY *is seated at left on a bench near the door.*

ROONEY (*To* NELLIE) Don't you know better than to go cruising Forty-second Street in broad daylight?

NELLIE Well, how's a person to make a living if she only works nights?

SERGEANT (*Consulting list*) Did you say Annie Burns or Nellie Burns?

NELLIE Nellie.

SERGEANT Don't see no check mark next to Nellie Burns for this week.

NELLIE I paid my five bucks.

SERGEANT Don't see no check mark. Sorry!

NELLIE I tell you I paid. You ask Willie Frye.
(*There is an outburst among the prostitutes seated on the bench*)

29

MARGIE (*To the girl on her right. Angry*) Put your head on his shoulder!
(*She shoves the girl's head from her shoulder*)

GIRL (*Sleepy*) Ah, Lillie.

NELLIE (*At* SERGEANT's *desk*) He come around collecting last Monday, and I give him my five bucks.

COP (*Enters and crosses to* TOMMY) The Lieutenant says what do you want?

TOMMY (*Rising*) I want to speak to him personally.

COP He says to tell you you can speak to me personally.

TOMMY I want to do him a favor. It's very important.

PROSTITUTE (*On bench at side*) I told you to put your head on him!
(*A drunk, dozing on the bench, comes awake and sings a few bars*)

SECOND PROSTITUTE (*To girl who has shoved her aside on bench*) Oh, Margie!

ROONEY (*To girls on bench*) Shut up, both of youse!
(*Ad lib confusion from group on bench.* WILLIE FRYE, *a plain-clothes detective, enters from the rear*)

FRYE Hey! (*Group on bench becomes silent at once*) Somebody want to get a broken head out here?

NELLIE (*Turning from* SERGEANT's *desk*)   Listen, you damn fly-cop! I paid you my five bucks! (FRYE *gives her a steely look. She changes to pleading*) Oh, please, Mr. Frye, you wouldn't cheat your pal Nellie. I paid you once.
(FRYE *pushes* NELLIE *aside*)

TOMMY (*Taking* FRYE *by the elbow and leading him downstage right*)   Willie, I got to see the Pantata.

SERGEANT (*At desk*)   Next!

FRYE   This is no time, Tommy. It's collection day.

TOMMY   I want to warn him about something. Go on. Tell him I got to warn him.
(LIEUTENANT SCHMIDT *enters*)

ROONEY (*Taking another girl to desk*)   Violet Dugan.

FRYE (*To* SCHMIDT)   That guy's still here.

SCHMIDT   Which one?

FRYE (*Pointing toward* TOMMY)   Over there.

TOMMY (*Eager, to* SCHMIDT)   Lieutenant—I'm Tommy Howatt.

SCHMIDT   What do you want?

TOMMY   I want to do you a favor. I come down to warn you.

SCHMIDT (*Bored*)   Okay, warn me.

31

TOMMY   The Reverend Andrew Brock is on his way over here.
(SERGEANT *rises and crosses out of cage*)

SCHMIDT (*Aroused*)   The preacher?

TOMMY   Yeah.

SCHMIDT   What for?

TOMMY   To have a showdown with you.

SCHMIDT   He's comin' here?

TOMMY   Yes, he is.

SCHMIDT   How do you know?

TOMMY   He told me.

SCHMIDT   He told you?

TOMMY   I thought if I was going to be appreciated by you, Lieutenant—if I was ever going to get cut in on any of the gravy—I better show that I could be useful.

FRYE (*In* SCHMIDT's *ear*)   This is the guy that sings at Clark's, Lieutenant.

TOMMY (*Following the worriedly pacing* SCHMIDT)   So I got me a job singing at the Old Stone Church, see? So I could keep track of things for you. (SCHMIDT *looks at* FRYE) The Reverend Brock is sort of my pal already.

SCHMIDT   That preacher is on his way here?

TOMMY   Sure—three o'clock—right away—he's comin'—I tried to warn you sooner, but—

SCHMIDT (*Sharp*)   Sergeant, get out in front and keep your eye peeled. (SERGEANT *exits.* SCHMIDT *strikes his forehead*) Oh, this is all I need!

TOMMY   I kept trying to send word to you for half an hour.

SCHMIDT (*Distraught*)   I got crackpots sendin' me word thirty times a day.

TOMMY   He's coming right after the Mission Meeting. He told me that personally.

SCHMIDT (*To the heavens*)   How'm I going to know—?

TOMMY   Tommy Howatt's the name. (SERGEANT *runs in*) After this you'll recognize who I am.

SERGEANT (*Excited*)   Lieutenant, he's hitching up his horse, the preacher!

SCHMIDT (*Crossing into cage and sitting*)   Get them drunks out of here! (*To* TOMMY) Get over there!
        (*General confusion as police clear the room.* TOMMY *exits downstage at right*)

NELLIE (*As she is dragged out*)   Maybe that preacher is right —this place stinks.

OTHERS (*Speaking*) I got rights! What about habeas corpus?
You know it! Come on, you.

SCHMIDT (*Shouts*) And keep 'em quiet!

SERGEANT (*At door*) Here he is.
 (*The room is cleared and serene as* BROCK *enters*)

SCHMIDT (*Oily*) Good afternoon, sir.

BROCK I have come to speak to Lieutenant Schmidt.

SCHMIDT Yes, sir, speaking. (BROCK *crosses to desk*) And I
got the honor of addressing who?

BROCK Andrew Brock. Rector of the Old Stone Church.

SCHMIDT Well—Your Reverence, this is a privilege. (*Shakes
hands*) And a big surprise. This is my chief inspector, Detective Frye.

BROCK (*Glancing at* FRYE) Ah, my cup runneth over. (*Looks
around*) I've never been inside a station house before.

FRYE Well, it's sort of home to us.
 (*Commotion offstage. Sound of a club hitting a skull*)

BROCK (*Dry*) There's no place like home.
 (FRYE *and* SCHMIDT *look at each other, puzzled*)

SCHMIDT I'm sure that's a compliment. Now, what can I do
for you?

34

BROCK For me, nothing, Lieutenant Schmidt. For my parishioners, indeed for all the citizens of this city, a great deal.

SCHMIDT Yeah?

BROCK There are many flagrant breaches of law in your precinct, Lieutenant.

SCHMIDT Such as?

BROCK Prostitution—gambling—and every—

SCHMIDT Now, wait a minute, Your Reverence. I wouldn't tolerate that. Not for one minute. Not them kind of places, no, sir. You been misinformed.

BROCK Have you tried raiding to close them down? But that's a stupid question. If there are no brothels, what is there to raid?

SCHMIDT That's the exact situation in a nutshell, Your Reverence. I don't know about any such places.

BROCK In that case, I suggest that you investigate a house of ill repute called Spanish Anna's—just one block from my church.

SCHMIDT What was that name?

BROCK It purports to be a social club—but I have it on good authority that it is a brothel.

FRYE (*Amazed*) A brothel?

ROONEY (*Astonished*) A bad house?

SCHMIDT (*Hard*) You heard His Reverence.

FRYE (*Hasty*) Oh, I don't think so. We got nothin' like that—

SCHMIDT Mr. Frye and me is both new to the precinct, Your Reverence. Perhaps we'd better ask a couple of the older men. (*Turns to policemen*) Rooney! Sergeant!

ROONEY Yes, sir.

SERGEANT Yes, Lieutenant.

SCHMIDT You men know anything about a disorderly house named Spanish—ah—?

BROCK Anna's—on Twenty-third, just west of Sixth Avenue.

SERGEANT (*Thoughtful*) There's the widow Anna Lopez takes in a few lady boarders—

BROCK And just one block further down the street, there is an even more reprehensible establishment known as Clark's.

SCHMIDT Clark's, huh? (*To policemen*) How about Clark's?

SERGEANT (*Thinking hard*) Clark's? How do you spell it?

SCHMIDT C-l-a-r-k apostrophe s. (*To* BROCK) Right?

BROCK Perfect.

SERGEANT (*Shakes head*) There couldn't be nothing like that going on without me and Rooney knowing about it.

FRYE (*To* BROCK) Could it be, sir, your informant may have been drinking and got his facts wrong?

BROCK My informant is an honorable young man who does not drink.

SCHMIDT This is pretty bad news to me, Your Reverence, and if it's true, there's going to be something done about it. (*Stern, to the policemen*) I don't never allow nothin' like that where I'm in charge. Understand?

ROONEY Yes, sir, yes, Lieutenant. I'll go to the addresses and find out personally.

SCHMIDT See you do, and look around for other houses. And especially for suspicious-lookin' women.

ROONEY Yes, sir.

SCHMIDT (*Tough*) I've told you all from the start—I don't stand for no immorality in my precinct. So if there's anything shady going on, you'd better dig it up and report to me or you'll be walking a beat in Brooklyn.

BROCK I realize you have a difficult problem—

SCHMIDT (*Turning to* BROCK) We do, and I'll tell you something else, Your Reverence. Stories get exaggerated. These out-of-town fellows, visitin' firemen we call 'em, they come down here and they get drunk. They want to make excuses, so they blame the wicked city. All day long, I got to hear these stories. This woman approached me; that man picked my pocket; and then when I investigate it—what do I find? Ninety-one percent of nothing.

BROCK Nevertheless, Lieutenant, that does not—

SCHMIDT But I can promise I'm gonna take care of this matter you speak of. I'm gonna follow this through big.

BROCK Very good, Lieutenant. And I'd appreciate it if you'd let me know the results of your investigation.

SCHMIDT Yes, sir.
(BROCK *crosses to left*)

BROCK Thank you for your courtesy. (BROCK *passes* FRYE *as* FRYE *moves to right*) I shall be hearing from you?

SCHMIDT You will indeed. Yes, sir. (BROCK *exits*) The poor bastard, he don't know what time it is, does he? Willie, along about the end of the week, we better have a raid on Spanish Anna.

FRYE (*In alarm*) Close it up?

SCHMIDT Just for a couple of days. Just for the church-going public. (TOMMY *re-enters*. SCHMIDT *nods and puts out his hand*. TOMMY *takes it*) You're all right, boy. I can use you.

Blackout

SCENE 6

Precinct street.

BROCK *is standing in front of the Precinct door. He gets out a note book and looks at it, puts on his gloves, makes a note in his book.*

GERTIE *and two young streetwalkers enter downstage at right. They sing.*

GIRLS
Little Old New Yo ho ho ho ho hork
Little Old New Yo ho ho ho ho hork

GERTIE (*As she reaches center she points at* BROCK) Look! Ain't that him? Sure, that's the preacher!

FIRST STREETWALKER Yeah, that's right. I seen his picture once.

GERTIE He looks like a reformer, don't he?

SECOND STREETWALKER What does reformers look like?
(BROCK *exits downstage at left*)

GERTIE They look just like him.

GIRLS
Reform, reform
It's only a passing storm
No matter what

39

TENDERLOIN

A reformer says or does
Things stay the way they was
So sweep us underneath the carpet
Keep us out of sight
Let reform have its day
We'll be back tomorrow night.

Reform, reform
Whenever it gets too warm
We hide inside our rooms
And count to ten
Then hit the streets again
When will reformers ever learn
Reform is hard to sell
'Cause in Little Old New York
No one gives a hoot in Hell!

GERTIE

    Little Old New Yo ho ho ho ho hork

FIRST STREETWALKER

    Little Old New Yo ho ho ho ho hork

SECOND STREETWALKER

    Little Old New Yo ho ho ho ho ho hork.

Blackout

SCENE 7

The living room in LAURA CROSBIE'S *opulently furnished Fifth Avenue house.*

LAURA *and* JESSICA *are seated side by side on a sofa.* JESSICA *is reading from a newspaper.*

JESSICA   "Lieutenant William Schmidt took personal charge of the raid. He later expressed his satisfaction with his success and hoped that this action would serve as stern warning that no disorderly house would be allowed to operate in his precinct." (*She stops reading and turns to* LAURA) Disorderly house. You know what that means, don't you?

LAURA   Of course I do.

JESSICA   A borde*loo*.

LAURA   (*Correcting her pronunciation*)   A bor*dello*.

JESSICA   A w-h-o-r-e house.

LAURA   Jessica, how do you know such words?

JESSICA   Don't you suppose I read the Bible? (*She reads*) "The men who were taken in the raid were permitted to go. But Mrs. Anna Lopez, known as Spanish Anna, and eleven

41

women in scanty attire were bundled into two patrol wagons and taken to Night Court."

(PURDY *has entered during the latter part of this*)

PURDY (*Incensed*)   Must you lend yourselves to such filth?

LAURA   But, Uncle Fred, it's a great triumph for Dr. Brock. Everyone is terribly excited about it.

PURDY   I'm not. I disapprove, and so do a great many other church members.

LAURA   Uncle Fred, there's never been such wonderful attendance in the history of the Old Stone Church.

PURDY   And I do not approve of some of the people who are being taken into the fold lately. Every afternoon now, you see Dr. Brock playing checkers with that young Howatt ruffian.

LAURA   He's not a ruffian, Uncle Fred.

PURDY   What is he?

LAURA   He's a nice bright boy who hasn't had opportunities, and I've invited him to tea this afternoon.

PURDY   Well, I never thought the day would come when a Bowery tough—we'll talk about this later, my girl.
(*He exits at right*)

JESSICA   Gee whiz. Men are certainly peculiar.

42

LAURA They're just afraid we'll know as much as they do.

JESSICA Laura, do you know about things? I mean about disorderly houses? I mean, I know men go down there to find women—

LAURA Mostly it's just adultery.

JESSICA Sure, and fornication.

LAURA Jessica, that's a terrible word.

JESSICA Oh, no, it's quite all right. Revelations: seventeen. Well, anyhow, it all means the same thing . . . though sometimes they call it sin and sometimes they call it "Sweet Mystery of Life."

TOMMY'S VOICE (*Offstage at left*) Is Miss Crosbie home?

BRIDGET'S VOICE (*Offstage at left*) Oh, yes indeed, Mr. Howatt. (JESSICA, *flustered, exits hurriedly at right*) You're expected.

LAURA (*Toward left*) Oh, there he is.

TOMMY'S VOICE I'll find my own way, Bridget.
     (TOMMY *enters*)

LAURA (*Crosses toward left*) Good afternoon, Mr. Howatt.

TOMMY Railroad time, huh? Right on the dot.

LAURA We have a friend. (*She turns toward where* JESSICA *was*) Oh, she was here. I guess she's gone for the tea.

TOMMY Well, I'll tell you how it is with me, Miss Crosbie. (*Strolling downstage to right*) I don't mind being alone with you. I can bear up under that.

LAURA Really?

TOMMY Dr. Brock sends regards. We been playing checkers. I just took his shirt—I mean, I defeated him.

PURDY'S VOICE (*Shouting offstage right*) It's a ridiculous, damnable situation!

LAURA Uncle Fred is in a terrible mood.

TOMMY I'm in such a good mood, I wouldn't notice.

JESSICA (*Entering downstage right with tea cart*) Here's the tea.

LAURA Oh, thank you, Jessica.

PURDY'S VOICE (*Grumbling offstage right*) Where are those confounded papers? Laura, you told me you knew where they were!

JESSICA (*Hasty*) I know where they are. I'll get them. (*She exits hurriedly downstage at right*)

TOMMY That uncle of yours don't like me—doesn't like me.

LAURA Dr. Brock does.

TOMMY Dr. Brock talked to me very intimate today. Told me about how his wife died. You know what he said to me?

Maurice Evans as REVEREND BROCK

He said I was kind of like a son to him. Could you believe that?

LAURA You should feel very flattered. Sugar?

TOMMY (*Picks up tongs curiously*) Hey, that's quite an idea. (*Drops lump in cup. Splash*) I guess the Reverend Brock can see I'm a sincere type of person and that's the reason he likes me. You think so?

LAURA No, Mr. Howatt. That's not what I think. Milk?
(*He nods*)

TOMMY If I was to tell you you—was—were—was—my ideal —what would you think?

LAURA I would think you ought to know me a little better before you reached any such rash conclusion.

TOMMY We've been sitting together in the choir for five days. Pretty close, too. How'd you like the way I crowded in next to you? (*She disapproves and sips tea*) Never mind, don't tell me. No, look, Laura—I mean Miss Crosbie. I always think of you as Laura, so it just slipped out. No, look, let's get personal. What do you like about me worst, and what do you like about me best?

LAURA I like you best when you sing. And I like you worst when you tell those outrageous lies.

TOMMY Lies, Miss Crosbie? Me? Name one.

LAURA The many society people you're intimate friends with?

TOMMY (*Abashed*) Oh, that . . .

LAURA And, uhhh . . .

TOMMY (*Rueful*) How about my father, the Mayor? That was the worst. He was really the town drunk. Well, I'll tell you, if you don't like those lies I'll cut down on them. (*Takes an envelope out of his pocket*) Look. Here's something I want you to have. This is sincere.

LAURA What is it?

TOMMY I couldn't sleep last night. So I wrote a little verse dedicated to you.

LAURA (*Pleased*) You did?

TOMMY Here.
    (*Passes it to her*)

LAURA Should I read it now?

TOMMY Sure. Read it out loud.
    (*She gives him her cup and takes out the poem*)

LAURA (*Reads aloud*) "To the prettiest girl in the choir":
    "She walks in beauty, like the night
    Of cloudless climes and starry skies
    And all that's best of dark and bright
    Meet in the aspect of her eyes."

TOMMY That last line was a tough one. I couldn't quite decide whether "Meet in her aspect *and* her eyes" or "Meet in the aspect *of* her eyes."

46

LAURA (*Indignant*) Honestly!

TOMMY (*Surprised*) You don't like it?

LAURA I like it very much!

TOMMY (*Smug*) I thought it was pretty good.

LAURA Lord Byron thought so, too!

TOMMY (*Deflated*) Oh.

LAURA (*Indignant*) One of the most famous poems in the world! Honestly, sometimes . . .

TOMMY Miss Crosbie, I ain't used to educated people. I tried that on some other girls and they thought it was fine.

LAURA (*Furious*) That has the ring of truth, at last.

TOMMY Miss Crosbie—Laura—where would I be if I stuck to the truth all the time?

LAURA I hope you'd be a real person called "Tommy."

TOMMY Well, I'll try.
     (*music*)

LAURA (*Singing*)
    Tommy, Tommy, when will you
    Begin to understand?
    I prefer you as you are
    To Byron second-hand.

If you like me
Say it simply,
"Laura, I like you."

TOMMY
Laura, I like you.

LAURA
Tommy, Tommy, if you can
Please drop the little boy
And let the nice young man come through.

TOMMY Well, maybe I will.
(JESSICA *enters*)

PURDY (*Roars offstage at right*) Maybe we'd better put a sign
up out in front. "Bowery Bums Welcome Here."

TOMMY (*With a chuckle*) Looks like the welcome sign has
just been taken off the mat. So the nice young man better
hit the road. I mean, I had better bid you adear—that don't
sound right. Someday you got to learn me to speak French.
Maybe English first, huh? Good-bye.
(*He exits at left*)

LAURA (*Singing*)
Tommy, Tommy, you don't know
This girl you think you see
Cool and calm and self-contained
And not a bit like me
You confuse me, you disturb me
More than I can say.

TENDERLOIN

Tommy, you don't know, or do you?
Something slowly draws me to you
Closer every day.

Blackout

Scene 8

Street in front of Clark's.

NELLIE *enters at left as two swells enter at right. The swells meet* NELLIE *at center, ignore her, and continue off at left.*

JOE *enters at right and meets* NELLIE *at center as two drunks enter at right. One is a bum; the other is elegantly attired.*

JOE *tips his hat to* NELLIE *and her admirer sits down with a thump at right center.*

NELLIE *meets the dressy drunk, solicits, but he passes out cold on the ground at right center.*

JOE, *astonished by the spectacle, points out the drunks to* SERGEANT, *who has entered at left.* SERGEANT *threatens him.*

JOE *exits hastily at left as a cop enters at right.* SERGEANT *motions to the cop to pick up the bum.*

They throw the drunken bum across the dressy drunk and carry them off at right, like a couple of logs.

SCENE 9

Clark's, a gaudily decorated, popular Tenderloin haunt.

At rise, there is much noise, laughter, and carousing. WILLIE
FRYE *is organizing a horse race with two prostitutes mounted
on shoulders of two male customers.*

CROWD (*Calling out*)
Come on, Lilly—!
Come on, Pearl—!
Give him the spurs—!
Even money on the red garters!

PEARL (*To man on whom she is mounted*) Don't start so
quick, you'll throw me off!

MARGIE (*To her mount*) Giddy up, horsie; giddy up, horsie!

PEARL (*Patting head of her mount*) Steady boy, steady boy!
(*Racers make a false start.* JOE KOVACK *enters downstage
at left*)

FRYE (*To riders*) Wait for the gate!

MAGGIE (*She pokes her head out of an upper tier. She is naked*)
Hey! Who won?
(*A man pulls her back*)

51

GERTIE (*Approaching* JOE) Looking for some fun?

JOE (*Nervous*) No, no, just mooching around.

GERTIE Well, you might buy me a drink.

FRYE They're off!
(*The couples race around the table.* JOE, *trapped, runs ahead of them.* NITA *pulls him out of the way into a booth at downstage right*)

NITA Look out, sport, you'll get run over.
(*Cheers for the winner as the race finishes*)

FRYE The winner gets a double eagle!
(*He hands the winner a twenty-dollar gold piece*)

JOE (*Dazed*) They keep goin' around.

NITA (*Laughs*) Yeah, that's the idea.

LIZ (*The Madam*) Hey, Margie! Come on, get up there!
(MARGIE *climbs on center table and begins to sing "Artificial Flowers"*)

JOE (*Looks at* MARGIE, *then turns to* NITA) Can I talk to you?

NITA Got a double eagle? Twenty dollars?

JOE Yes, ma'am.

NITA Good. Then we can have a drink.

52

JOE I don't drink much.

NITA Bet you could if you wanted too, though, huh? How about some champagne?

JOE Yes, ma'am.

NITA (*To* WAITER) Hey, Jake, champagne!

MAGGIE (*Still naked. She pokes her head out of upper tier*) Hey, who won the race?

MAN (*Pulls her back*) Come back here. Hey, Margie, shut up. Let Tommy sing.

MARGIE (*Thumbing her nose up at him*) This is for you.

GIRL (*Doing the same*) Yeah, this is for you!

JOE Ha, ha, ha, there sure is lots going on.

NITA That's why I always charge a double eagle for my time.

JOE Oh, I got the money. Don't worry.
   (*He gives her a twenty-dollar bill*)

NITA (*Looking at his roll*) What'd you do—sell the cow? (*Calls*) Gertie, what do you think of my new lover?
   (GERTIE *makes a face.* TOMMY *enters downstage at left. He is dressed in the style of a dandy of the period*)

GIRL Here he is, here's Tommy.

LIZ Tommy, you're late.

TOMMY How do you like my new suit?

LIZ Earn your money. Get up there.

TOMMY (*Heading for the table at center*) Sure, glad to oblige.
(*He jumps up onto the table*)

TOMMY (*Singing*)
Shame, shame, shame, shame

MARGIE
Shame, shame, shame, shame

TOMMY
He was utterly dissolute, sensual, wicked and sly
She was utterly virtuous, virginal, sheltered and shy
He had to have this proper young maid
And so his plans were properly laid
This malicious old, vicious old, lecherous, treacherous guy.

TOMMY *and* MARGIE
He fed (he fed)
Her lobster (her lobster)
And sparkling wine (and sparkling wine)
That crafty old swine (that crafty old swine)
Her head began to swim (her head began to swim)
Which was no surprise to him (which was no surprise to him)
And then (and then)
And then (and then)
He gratified his whim!

TOMMY

> Since that lecherous bounder
> Got 'round her and led her astray
> She's the picture of happiness
> Laughing and singing all day
> There are roses in her cheeks now
> People listen when she speaks now
> No one like her since the days of Salome!
>
> From a simple beginning
> Just see how her sinning has paid
> She's the picture of happiness
> Now that she's mastered a trade.

CHORUS

> Shame, shame, shame, shame
> Shame, shame, shame, shame

TOMMY

> Here's an even more delicate, innocent maiden I know
> Who attracted an eminent, elegant, elderly beau
> He was aflame with primitive lust
> And so he vowed that have her he must
> It's a typical, tragical story of worry and woe.

TOMMY *and* CHORUS

> The cad (the cad)
> He promised (he promised)
> That they would wed (that they would wed)
> That's just what he said (that's just what he said)
> His purpose he concealed (his purpose he concealed)
> While he led her far afield (while he led her far afield)
> And then (and then)

And then (and then)
He tempted her to yield.

TOMMY

Since that lecherous bounder
Got 'round her and led her astray
She's the picture of happiness
Laughing and singing all day
There are roses in her cheeks now
People listen when she speaks now
No one like her since the days of Salome!

From a simple beginning
Just see how her sinning has paid
She's the picture of heavenly happiness
Now that she's made . . .
The grade . . .
The picture of happiness
Now that she's mastered a trade.

DEACON (*Entering*) Any policemen raidin' this joint tonight?
(*Ad lib laughs*)

LIZ Don't say such things, Deacon. You give me the shakes.

FRYE There won't be no more raids, Liz.

LIZ I hope not.

FRYE That one ought to keep the Reverend Brock happy for
a couple of years.

TENDERLOIN

DEACON Got some dandy pictures in that raid. Got one of Old Anna kickin' a cop right in the face.

GERTIE You wouldn't make dirty pictures, would you, Deacon?

DEACON I'm an artist—I'll do anything for money.
(GERTIE *tells* NITA TOMMY *is here*)

NITA (*Crossing out of booth at right*) Hey, scoop!

TOMMY (*Showing off his new clothes*) How ya like it? I always wanted a pair of these Plymouth Rock pants.

NITA Who's keepin' you?

TOMMY This is honest money, Tootsie. I'm gettin' a percentage from the Pantata.

JOE (*Looking at* TOMMY) I know him.

NITA (*To* JOE) Oh, be quiet.
(NITA *closes curtains of booth*)

TOMMY (*Strutting*) This is the very latest.
(NITA *walks past* JOE *with* TOMMY)

JOE (*Coming out of booth*) He goes to my church.

NITA (*Stops and turns*) He does what?

JOE Sure. He's the one that sings so pretty. Don't you know

me, mister? I was at the Parish House with the Reverend
Brock—remember?

TOMMY (*Looking at him more closely*) Oh, sure. How are
you?

JOE You sung about Little Annie and the flowers and I even
remember your name—Tommy Howatt.

TOMMY Oh.

JOE My name is Joe Kovack.

TOMMY Sure. Well, glad to see you once again, Brother Kovack.

JOE Me, too, Brother Howatt.

NITA (*Dry*) Let us pray.

TOMMY Ain't this kind of an unusual place for you to be
found at, Brother Kovack?

JOE I ain't done nothin'—I'm just lookin'.

NITA (*To* GERTIE) Gert! (*To* JOE) Go in there and have some
fun with Flirty Gertie for a while, will you, Brother Kovack?
(GERTIE *goes toward booth at right*)

JOE But suppose I was to tell the Reverend Brock I seen you?

TOMMY That might get you in a lot of trouble, but it wouldn't
hurt me. I sing here.

NITA   Go with Gertie. I'll join you later.

JOE   I want to stay here.

NITA   (*Angry*)   Skidaddle. Geez, be nice.

GERTIE   (*Pulling* JOE *into booth*)   Come on, sport. Come on—you'll get used to me. I got hidden talents.

NITA   That's very interesting—you singing at that church.

TOMMY   That's how I get my cut from the Pantata. I wise him up what's goin' on. And then I also wise up the Reverend Brock what's goin' on in the Tenderloin. I'm a benefit to everybody. Understand?

NITA   I guess so. It ain't only the double cross, it's the *double* double cross. And you told me you was gonna take me for a buggy ride.

TOMMY   When did I?

NITA   Why, you don't even remember, you stinker!
(*She pummels him*)

LIZ   (*Crossing between them*)   Hey, hey, hey, keep it sweet and lovely. Where do you think you are? Don't make no trouble.
(*She shoves* TOMMY *away*)

NITA   (*Shouts after him*)   I'll fix your Holy Roller friend . . .

TOMMY   (*Crossing on his way out at left*)   *My* friend?

NITA Yeah, *your* friend. Has he ever had a mickey?
(TOMMY *exits*)

GERTIE (*Coming out of booth with money*) Yes, he has. He just had one—and he loves them.

FRYE (*Approaching* GERTIE, *leering at her money*) What do you do, print that stuff?

GERTIE I told you I was a thirty-dollar girl.

FRYE Let me know when you get marked down.
(*They dance*)

GERTIE (*Bargaining with him*) Twenty dollars?—Fifteen? (*He is indifferent*) Ten! (FRYE *and* GERTIE *circle table*) Five? —Three?— How about a dollar thirty?— My treat!

Blackout

SCENE 10

Street in front of Clark's.

A drunken JOE KOVACK *staggers across the stage from left to right, and is led away roughly by a cop.*

61

Scene 11

A beach.

At rise, PURDY *is seated at left in a beach chair, reading the* Wall Street Journal. *Singing is heard offstage right. Two pretty girls in bathing suits are seated, upstage center, on a blanket with a large picnic basket.*

LAURA *and friends enter downstage left, joining in the singing of "My Miss Mary," and cross upstage to the blanket.* LAURA *carries a camera and poses the group for a picture as* BROCK *and others enter upstage left.*

All, except PURDY, *wear colorful bathing costumes of the period.*

BROCK (*To* MARTIN *and group as they exit downstage right*) Enjoy yourselves, children. Have a good time. (*Pounds his ear to shake out water*). Beautiful, beautiful day, and such a good thing for us all to get away from all our problems.

PURDY The market went down again yesterday.

BROCK Well, I doubt whether I can be held responsible for that, Brother Purdy, and I doubt if Wall Street has shares in Spanish Anna's.

62

PURDY (*Dry*) You might be surprised.

BROCK What!

PURDY Somebody owns the real estate in the Tenderloin.

BROCK Not you, I hope.

PURDY (*Laughs*) I am joking, Dr. Brock. They don't take your attacks seriously.

BROCK But they will. This one raid on the Spanish Anna place is only the beginning. The police will gradually ferret them out one by one and close them down . . .

JESSICA (*Entering downstage left with girl friend*) I found a seashell.
    (*They collect at stage center*)

BROCK The Tenderloin may not be dead, but it's dying.

PURDY Let me tell you something.

BROCK No, Brother Purdy, let me tell *you* something. (*He sings*)
    Dear friend, may I say
    This is much too nice a day
    To talk of that
    Not today
    When the beach is like a welcome mat.

    Be the boon companion
    Not the financier

TENDERLOIN

How can I be solemn
With water in my ear?

Dear friend, just relax
Let's enjoy ourselves
And be the best of friends
Take my word
This is what the doctor recommends.

See the way the ocean merges with the sky
Let's be like that, you and I
Dear friend, let's be dear friends.

GROUP

Dear friend, may I say
It's too nice a day to talk of this and that
Not today
When the world is like a welcome mat.

Worry is behind us
Work is far away
Why should we be solemn
On such a sunny day?

Dear friend, just relax
Let's enjoy ourselves
And be the best of friends
Take my word
This is what the doctor recommends.

See the way the ocean merges with the sky
Let's be like that, you and I
Dear friend, let's be

64

BROCK	GROUP
Dear friend . . .	Dear friend, may I say It's too nice a day to talk of this and that
Dear friend . . .	Not today When the world is like a welcome mat.

BROCK

Time is of the essence
Use it with a will
While the earth is turning
Should we be standing still?

(BROCK *dances with* LAURA, JESSICA, *and* JESSICA's *friend*)

GROUP

Like sky
And sea
You'll blend
With me
Dear friend,
Let's be
Dear friends.

(BROCK *ends the number by dropping breathless into the
beach chair, surrounded by the group*)

JOE (*Enters downstage right*) Dr. Brock? Can I talk to you?

BROCK (*Sees* JOE) Why, Brother Kovack, welcome. Do join
us. We haven't seen you for some days. Let's get you into a
bathing suit.

(BROCK *goes into a cabana at upstage left*)

65

JOE I . . . I can't stay long.

JESSICA (*Seashell at her ear*) Oh, Laura, oh, listen . . . You ought to hear this seashell. It's just wonderful. I can hear it so plain.

ECHO (*Resonant from offstage*) "Ah, life is a beautiful mystery, men, men, men."

JESSICA Listen, Mr. Kovack, just listen to it.
　　　(*She holds out the seashell. He puts it to his ear*)

ECHO (*Resonant from offstage*) "Sin, sin, wicked Joe Kovack, dirty Joe Kovack, the fires of hell."

JOE (*Hands back seashell*) Very pretty.
　　　(LAURA *snaps a picture of* JOE *and* JESSICA)

JESSICA Oh, Laura, I was a sight. Where did you get the camera?

LAURA It's Tommy's. He had to be late, so he asked me to get him some snaps.
　　　(BROCK *enters, carrying his bathing suit*)

BROCK Here we are, Brother Kovack.

LAURA Dr. Brock, will you pose for me, please?

BROCK Very willingly, my dear. Now what do you want—the orator, the friend, the reformer, or the winner of the hop, skip and jump?
　　　(*He poses.* LAURA *snaps the picture*)

LAURA Thank you.
(*Laughter offstage at right*)

JESSICA There's Tommy, come on.

JOE Reverend . . . Can I talk to you?

BROCK Yes, Brother Kovack, is something wrong? (JOE *nods*) Well, my good friend, let's just sit down and you tell me what it is.
(JOE *sits in the chair at left*)

JOE Reverend, I been in jail.

BROCK Oh, dear, what for?

JOE Drunk and disorderly.

BROCK My friend. My dear friend.
(*He puts his hand on* JOE's *shoulder*)

JOE I went down to one of those places. I thought I'd like to see what they was like before they was all closed up. And I went down there.

BROCK Yes?

JOE And there was women and fellows and there was one— her name was Nita—(BROCK *nods*) And I don't know how such a nice girl could be in a place like that, and I drank too much. And it's all kind of mixed up because pretty soon I was with Gertie.

67

BROCK   Gertie, too? Oh, dear!

JOE   I sinned, Reverend, with the wrong woman. I didn't want Gertie, I wanted Nita.

BROCK   (*Hands raised to be spared the details*)   Please! Please!

JOE   At least Gertie's the one I seen taking money out of my pants. I was awful sick, Reverend, but I seen her do it. She said I owed it to her and then I kind of forget what happened till the police took me away to the jail.

BROCK   We're none of us spotless, Brother Kovack, we all make mistakes—

JOE   I ain't finished, Reverend.

BROCK   You're not?

JOE   When I was in jail I heard 'em all talking about you.

BROCK   About me? In jail?

JOE   All about how you went to see this here Pantata. And he pulled the wool over your eyes, Reverend.

BROCK   He did what?

JOE   The guys in jail—they say he just had the police raid one joint to take you in, and now they're laughin' at you and everything is running full blast.

BROCK   This is false. (*Laughter offstage at right. Ad libs: "Hurry back," "Speed it up"*) I can't believe that!

68

TOMMY (*Backing onstage at right, talking to group offstage*) Sure, soon as I get my suit on, I'll join you.

BROCK Thomas!

TOMMY (*Turning*) Got a good day for it, eh, Dr. Brock?

BROCK May I speak to you? (TOMMY *crosses to* BROCK) You are my friend?

TOMMY I sure hope so.

BROCK And you would keep me well informed concerning any developments in the Tenderloin?

TOMMY (*Confused*) Well, I—I—

BROCK Is it wide open? Tell me the truth. (TOMMY *opens his mouth to lie*) The truth!

TOMMY (*Quiet*) Yes, sir. Wide open.

BROCK And the police are looking the other way?

JOE They opened Spanish Anna's again.

BROCK (*To* TOMMY) Is that true?

TOMMY That's true.

BROCK (*Grimly*) Thank you.
(*He stalks off at right with determination.* JOE *starts to follow him*)

69

JOE (*To* TOMMY) You look kind of unhappy, Brother Howatt.

TOMMY Do I, Brother Kovack? Well, how the hell do you think you look?
(*Exit* JOE *at right.* JESSICA, LAURA *and girl enter upstage at right and cross over*)

LAURA I thought you were going to put on your suit?

TOMMY Yeah, in just a minute. Oh, did you get some pictures for me?

LAURA (*Passing the camera*) Oh, yes.

JESSICA (*Simpering*) The worst of me you ever saw.
(JESSICA *and the other girl go out at left*)

TOMMY There's two left. Let me take one of you.

LAURA Tommy, is something the matter?

TOMMY No, no, not a thing. Come on, give me a pose. (*She stands waiting to have her picture taken*) Hold out your hands to me like you're supposed to like me.

LAURA I can do that.
(*She holds out her hands. He takes a picture and begins to plan another*)

TOMMY Now, let's see.
(*He poses her at left, arm up*)

TENDERLOIN

LAURA That's enough.

TOMMY I want one sitting down.

LAURA I don't want to sit down—I want to swim.
(TOMMY *grabs her by the arm*)

TOMMY One sitting down!

LAURA (*Laughing and resisting*) No.
(*They struggle. He wrestles with her and gets her to the ground. The intimate contact affects them both. There is a slight embarrassed pause. Then he retreats, picks up his camera, and takes a picture while she sits very still*)

TOMMY (*A little embarrassed*) Thanks for the pose.

LAURA (*Quietly*) You're very masterful—aren't you?

TOMMY (*Sits down beside her*) You have a terrible effect on me and I forget—that you are above me.

LAURA What a horrible thing to say.

TOMMY Might as well say it as think it.

LAURA Tommy, Tommy, Tommy, you're so bright and ambitious—you should feel you're superior. You don't have to call yourself Howatt the Second just because Ellington Smythe does.

TOMMY I've done better than that.
(*He passes her one of his calling cards*)

71

LAURA (*Reads aloud*) "Mr. Thomas Dubonnet Howatt the Third."
(*She looks at him*)

TOMMY (*Worried*) Too much, huh?

LAURA (*Passing back the card*) Where'd you get the Dubonnet?

TOMMY Off a bottle.
(BROCK *enters downstage at right*)

BROCK I want to speak to Thomas.

LAURA (*Picking up camera*) Oh, certainly.
(*She exits downstage at left*)

BROCK Tom, I have made a decision. I am going down to the Tenderloin personally to investigate.

TOMMY Gee whiz, Dr. Brock, you can't do that . . . that would be terrible. You don't know what it's like. I'm scared of what might happen.

BROCK So am I, Tommy. I'm scared, too. That's why I want you to be there.

TOMMY Me?

BROCK Friend or foe, Tom, which is it?

TOMMY Friend—every day in the week—you know that—but—

TENDERLOIN

BROCK Very well, you see, I know you sing at Clark's.

TOMMY Oh, you do?

BROCK Yes, Brother Kovack let that slip. I realize you know about these places. I need your help.

TOMMY You still trust me?

BROCK I still trust you.
(MARTIN *enters downstage at right*)

MARTIN Ready, sir.

BROCK Bring in the others.

MARTIN (*Calls offstage at right*) This way, men!
(*Four church stalwarts enter downstage at right and cross to* BROCK)

BROCK We shall cleave them with a two-edged sword. Gather round me, please. Napoleon had his old guard. I have you, my young guard. I'm going to ask you to volunteer for a duty which requires both mental and physical courage. Secret agents for the Army of Decency. We shall close the Tenderloin despite the police force. We shall close it by laying before the public itemized evidence of what goes on down there. Names, places, facts. We shall arouse public opinion so that the authorities will be forced to act. The Mayor—the Governor—I am going to get that evidence. I am going to visit these hell-holes personally. Are you with me? Who stands with Andrew Brock?

MARTIN I do!

FIRST STALWART Yes, sir!

SECOND STALWART I do!

THIRD STALWART I do!

BROCK Very well, we shall collect the data on this district sys-
tematically. Each one of you, two or three different places
every night of the week—and we start tonight. Thomas, what
time shall we foregather?

TOMMY Well, do you want to see it when it's—?

BROCK We want to see it when it's wide open!

TOMMY About eleven o'clock.

BROCK Then we'll meet in the vestry at ten-thirty.

TOMMY And you better dress up like—you know, disguise.

BROCK Oh, yes, everybody in disguise. Now, let me say one
thing further. There is a penalty attached to this enterprise.
We shall not complete this task without bringing extensive
criticism on our heads. We may come through with honor,
we may come through with disgrace. But I assure you that
any man who is willing to make this sacrifice may rest con-
tent that he has fought the good fight. That he has taken up
God's work. Now then, what is your answer?
    (*They sing*)

MARTIN
> With trumpet and timbrel, cymbal and harp

MARTIN *and* FIRST STALWART
> I shall march

MARTIN, FIRST *and* SECOND STALWARTS
> In the army

MARTIN *and* THREE STALWARTS
> Of the just
>> (BROCK *looks at* TOMMY)

> With trumpet and timbrel
> Cymbal and harp

TOMMY, MARTIN *and* MEN
> I shall march
> In the army of the just

BROCK *and* MEN
> To the pure shall the victory be given (given)
> From this earth shall iniquity be driven (driven)
> Overnight every sinner shall be shriven (shriven)

ALL
> By the army of the just.

BROCK *and* MEN
> For the Day of Judgment is at hand (is at hand)
> Yes, the Day of Judgment is at hand (is at hand)
> And virtue shall reign (virtue shall reign)
> Virtue shall reign (virtue shall reign).

ALL

 Virtue shall reign throughout the land.
  (They march, and as the clouds gather, their marching
  accelerates)

 With trumpet and timbrel, cymbal and harp
 I shall march in the army of the just
 With trumpet and timbrel, cymbal and harp
 I shall march in the army of the just.
 Let my faith lead the sinner to salvation
 Let my heart show the way to exaltation
 Let my soul be a great recruiting station
 For the army of the just.
  (They run off frantically ahead of an imminent rainfall)

   Blackout

SCENE 12

Street in front of Clark's.

As the lights come up, JOE *is seen crossing from left to right
on his way to Clark's.*

Clark's, 11:00 P.M., in full swing.

At rise, MARGIE *is standing on center table singing "Artificial Flowers."*

NELLIE (*Heard from booth at right in which a card game is in progress*) Hey, I beat the Deacon!
      (JOE *enters downstage at left and* GERTIE *dances over to him*)

GERTIE Here's my lover.

ELEGANT MAN (*Calls*) Ladies and gentlemen, my treat! Mumm's for everybody!

GIRL Oh, boy, champagne!

JOE (*Crossing to* NITA) I got to talk to you.
      (*He gets out money*)

GIRL (*Raising glass*) Here's to a true sport!
      (*Ad libs: "You bet!" "Drink up!"*)

NITA (*To* JOE) Sure. (*She puts money in top of her stocking*) Nice to see you lookin' so good.

JOE I wasn't never comin' back here, and then I was in my

78

room and I had a kind of dream, like a vision, only terrible real, and you was there standin' all white holdin' your hands out like you wanted me to help you.

NITA Listen, farmer . . .

JOE My name is Joe.

NITA Listen, Joe. (*She leans on table*) We gave you a mickey . . . do you know that? (*She sits*) You've been given a kind of rough goin' over. (JOE *sits*) This vision'll go away in a couple of days.

JOE You ain't in no trouble?

NITA I can take care of myself.

JOE I brung you a present.

NITA You did? Why?

JOE I ain't never going to see you again—(*Hands box to her*) —so I might as well tell you. I know I ain't nothing to you, but I'm in love with you. When I was a boy sixteen years old, there was a girl in our town—and we got mixed up and —you know—and then she says that I'm responsible—and after that I never had nothing to do with women.
   (GERTIE *passes*)

GERTIE (*To* NITA) Telling him how you lost it?

NITA Ugh-ugh, he's telling me. (*Opens box as* GERTIE *passes on*) Ah, gee, a cut-glass ring. Just what I always wanted.

79

JOE (*Rising*) That ain't glass. That's a diamond.

NITA (*Rising*) It couldn't be: it's too big. (*She holds it to her cheek. Looks at him amazed*) But I thought you was a farmer?

JOE I am. But they found coal under my farm.

NITA (*Takes* JOE *by the arms*) You mean you got a coal mine? You're rich, huh? You don't act like it.

JOE I ain't used to it yet.

NITA (*Puts on ring*) I never had nothin' so wonderful in my whole life. My God, ain't you the sweet fella.
(*She kisses him, puts her arms around him and hugs him*)

DEACON (*At card game in booth*) Come on—pay the Deacon!

JOE Well, I know it's no good me being in love with you, so I'm going away somewhere till I get over it. If you're ever in any trouble you can sell that, see? Good-bye forever.
(*He starts out*)

NITA Joe. (*He stops*) Why do you have to go so quick? Can't you wait a day or so?

JOE I gotta think. I'm all mixed up.

NITA Why don't you come back tomorrow? Just one more day. For me? Please?

JOE All right, I will.

NITA I'll be lookin' for you. (JOE *exits*) Gertie—I got me a millionaire! (JOE *runs back in, looks around frantically, rushes into booth at left. A scream is heard.* BROCK *and two of his stalwarts enter at left and walk to center, looking around apprehensively. When they pass the booth,* JOE *tumbles out and starts crawling off left.* BROCK *and his men are disguised as their version of "sports"—wild plaid suits, plus fours, cowboy hats.* NITA *calls*) Joe! Joe! Joe!

JOE (*Frightened*) Shhh! Shhh!
     (JOE *exits on hands and knees at left*)

LIZ What's the matter with him?
     (GIRL *dances with* BROCK *at center*)

MARGIE (*To* MARTIN) Want to buy me a drink?

MARTIN (*Nervous, referring to* BROCK) Ask him.

MARGIE (*To* BROCK) Does he want to buy me a drink?

BROCK (*Broad accent*) You betcha!

MARGIE (*Calls*) Jake! Champagne!

BROCK (*Hasty*) No, not champagne. Just beer.

MARGIE (*Disgusted*) Ah, one of those, huh? Good-bye.

NELLIE (*Approaching* BROCK) Hey, mister, you could buy me a beer if you wanted to.

TENDERLOIN

BROCK (*Backing away*) I think I'll take a little look around first.

NELLIE Cheapskate!

GIRL (*To* MARTIN) Want to go upstairs?

MARTIN I don't think so.

BROCK (*Sharp, to* MARTIN) Did that woman say "upstairs"?

MARTIN Yes, sir.

BROCK Find out what she means and make a note of it.

MARTIN Oh, I know what she means.

BROCK So do I. But make a note of it. We want facts and figures.
>(ANOTHER GIRL *leans out of upstairs booth and flirts with* BROCK)

ANOTHER GIRL Hey, Daddy—Come on up!
>(TOMMY *enters at left, exchanges look with* BROCK *and men*)

NITA (*Sarcastic*) Look who's giving us the honor!

LIZ Yeah—on his night off, too.

TOMMY I thought I'd see what was going on.

NITA Here's what's going on. (*Shows ring*) Get an eyeful of that.

82

TOMMY Cute.

NITA You're damn right it's cute. It's real.
(MARGIE *steals a stalwart's purse*)

STALWART Hey, come back here. Give me that pocketbook,
you little thief!

MARGIE (*Returning pocketbook*) Can't you take a joke?

STALWART Just keep your hands off me.

LIZ You lookin' for trouble? (*To cop*) Rooney!

TOMMY (*Hurries over and pushes cop aside*) Come on, he's
just a greenhorn. Leave him alone.

GIRL (*Starting leapfrog game*) All right, you're first. Hey,
pal, watch those hands.
(*Boys play leapfrog over the girls.* BROCK *joins in*)

GIRL Look at that old goat go!
(BROCK *jumps over the last girl and makes a note in his
book*)

FRYE (*To* BROCK) Excuse me, mister. I been watching you
write a good deal of stuff in that book.

BROCK Indeed I ha . . . (*Correcting accent*) You betcha!

FRYE What's the idea?

BROCK It's so I can remember what a good time I'm having.

83

FRYE Let's have a look. (*Takes book and reads aloud*) "Girls painted—solicitations—embraces—want to go upstairs" (BROCK *digs him in the ribs*) "Nudity—depravity—strong drink"
(*He gives* BROCK *the book*)

LIZ Speakin' of strong drink, I ain't seen you buy any.

BROCK Oh, I'm going to.

LIZ Good. (*Calls to* WAITER) Champagne for this gent.

FRYE (*Crossing around* BROCK) Ain't I seen you some place before?

BROCK Well, now lemme see—maybe—I oughter remember a handsome feller like you. Race track?

FRYE Ah, the races, huh? Where at?

BROCK Saratoga, maybe?

FRYE By God, you're right. Saratoga, six years ago. (*They shake hands*) I never forget a face. Have fun.

NITA (*Moving out of group at left*) I told you already, it's real. (*She sings*)
Oh, it's grand how the money changes hands

MAN You tell 'em, Nita.

NITA
Yes, it's grand how the money changes hands
Everybody's happy
That's the way she stands

LEFT GROUP

Just as long as the money changes hands.
(MARTIN, *who has been listening to the song, becomes aware that one of the girls is attempting to pick his pocket. He thrusts her hand aside*)

MARTIN (*Angry*) Oh, no you don't.
(MARTIN *and a stalwart move away from the girls at the table and join* BROCK *at right*)

MAN Once more, baby!

NITA

You got to pay the dentist for a tooth he's gonna yank
So you go and get some money from the bank

LEFT GROUP

From the bank

NITA

So you pay the dentist
And he pays

LEFT GROUP

The landlord

NITA

The landlord pays

LEFT GROUP

The grocer

NITA

The grocer pays

85

LEFT GROUP
> The farmer

NITA
> The farmer pays

LEFT GROUP
> The banker

NITA
> The banker spends it here!

NITA *and* LEFT GROUP
> Tra-la-la-la-la-la
> Everybody's happy
> That's the way she stands
> Just as long as the money changes hands.
>> (LEFT GROUP *laughs. The* WAITER *crosses to* BROCK *and the men at right with a tray of champagne and glasses*)

WAITER   Twenty dollars.
> (BROCK *and men dig worriedly to make the twenty dollars.* MARTIN *gives the money to the* WAITER *and takes the tray as* LIZ *sings*)

LIZ
> You get so much enjoyment
> From a bottle of champagne
> That it's fun to pour your money
> Down the drain

RIGHT GROUP
> Down the drain
> So you pay the waiter

WAITER
> And I pay the boss
> (BROCK *and the men move upstage right with the tray*)

RIGHT GROUP
> Oh, it's grand how the money changes hands.

LIZ
> The boss pays the grocer
> The grocer pays

RIGHT GROUP
> The farmer

LIZ
> The farmer pays

RIGHT GROUP
> The banker

LIZ
> The banker spends it here!

LIZ *and* RIGHT GROUP
> Tra-la-la-la-la-la
> Everybody's happy
> That's the way she stands
> Just as long as the money changes hands.

GERTIE
> Oh, the men pay the girls

GIRL
> And the girls pay Liz

GERTIE *and* GIRLS
> Oh, it's grand how the money changes hands.

BROCK
> So the men pay the girls

GIRLS
> And the girls pay Liz

ANOTHER GIRL
> Yeah, we pay her

MARGIE
> And she pays the cops!

GIRLS
> Oh, it's grand how the money changes hands

ALL
> Yes, it's grand how the money changes hands
> Everybody's happy
> That's the way she stands
> Just as long as the money changes hands.

BROCK (*To* FRYE)
> So Liz pays the cops

FRYE
> And the cops pay me

BROCK *and* FRYE
> Oh, it's grand how the money changes hands.

BROCK (*To* FRYE)
> So the cops pay you

FRYE
> And I pay Schmidt

LIZ
> And Schmidt pays the Alderman

ALL
> And the Alderman pays the Mayor
> Tra-la-la-la-la-la
> Everybody's happy
> That's the way she stands
> Just as long as the money changes hands.

BROCK
> So the men pay

GERTIE
> The girls

BROCK
> And the girls pay

GIRL
> Liz

BROCK
> And Liz pays

MARGIE
> The cops

TENDERLOIN

BROCK
> And the cops pay

GIRLS
> Frye

BROCK
> And Frye pays

ALL
> Schmidt

BROCK
> And Schmidt pays

ALL
> The Alderman

BROCK
> And the Alderman pays

ALL
> The Mayor
> Tra-la-la-la-la-la
>   (BROCK *signals his men to go*)
>
> Everybody's happy
> That's the way she stands
> Just as long as the money changes hands.

BROCK   So long, chums . . . see you in church!

90

TENDERLOIN

ALL

Just as long as the money
Changes . . . hands . . .
(BROCK *exits with his men*)

Curtain

Wynne Miller and Ron Husmann as LAURA and TOMMY

ACT TWO

SCENE I

Central Park.

There are benches on either side in the foreground, a bridle path and bridge in the rear. JOE *is sitting on a bench at right, staring into space. A couple of horseback riders cross on the path, riding hobby horses.*

PURDY *enters hurriedly at left. He lifts his hat and greets the riders. He looks after the riders as though seeking someone— and then sees* JOE.

PURDY   Joe, have you seen my niece?

JOE   Huh?

PURDY *(Irritably)*   My ward. Laura.

JOE   Oh, I don't think so.

PURDY   Why aren't you with the others? What are you doing here by yourself?

JOE   I'm struggling with my soul.
    ("My Miss Mary" is heard offstage at left)

PURDY   Joe. What's the matter with you?
    *(*BROCK *and* MARTIN *enter at left, heads down, talking*

95

They walk sedately toward right, absorbed in their conversation)

BROCK   The fact that the Governor asked to read a verbatim report of yesterday's sermon—that is the encouraging thing.

MARTIN   *(Troubled)*   If he would only act—

BROCK   We'll force someone to act. I'll give them another broadside next Sunday.
   (They go out at right)

PURDY   Did you hear Dr. Brock's sermon yesterday?

JOE   No, Brother Purdy, I didn't. I was struggling with my soul yesterday, too.

PURDY   *(Beside himself)*   The details of the visits of members of our church to the worst dives in this city! Sexual orgies dished up in the most lurid manner! The names and addresses of dozens of these places! Klondike Katie's! House of All Nations! Sixteen to One Club! Friendly Flora's! Spanish Anna's! Little Egypt!

JOE   You sure know the names all right.
   (Laughter off. MRS. BARKER, an older church lady, and others enter at left as BROCK and MARTIN return, strolling in from right)

MRS. BARKER   Dr. Brock—we're going to play spoons—now, you must join us.

BROCK   Sister Barker, you know how I love these games—but today, with so much on my mind—
   (*The group gathers around* BROCK. *Upstage, on bridle-path,* LAURA *and* TOMMY *ride in on hobby horses from left.* ELLINGTON *rides in from right. They are posting*)

LAURA   Hello, Ellington.

ELLINGTON   Hello, Laura.
   (*They ride out at right. "My Miss Mary" is heard faintly. In the meantime* JESSICA *has run in breathlessly from downstage right*)

JESSICA   Dr. Brock, there's a policeman looking for you!

BROCK   What?

JESSICA   (*Breathless*)   He came to the Parish House. He said it's important. There was another man with him. He said—

BROCK   Now, Jessica, just calm yourself. What kind of a policeman?

JESSICA   A big one—with gold things on his collar.

BROCK   (*Quick*)   And the other man was a rather slinky type with red hair?

JESSICA   (*Nods*)   Is it bad?

BROCK   Bad? No, no, Jessica—it's good. (*Shouts*) Victory!

97

TENDERLOIN

(Music. Others come in to find out what is going on when MRS. BARKER *waves to them)* At last! Victory!

MARTIN   Dr. Brock, do you think—?

BROCK   I think it means that the Governor has acted—that I have won—that they have come hat in hand to beg for mercy.

MARTIN   What will you do?

BROCK   Do? What God wills. For the moment I can only rejoice. My friends, my good companions, we have done our work. Now we may rejoice.

MRS. BARKER   Oh, Dr. Brock, it's good to see you so happy.

BROCK   Happy—I'm free! Now I'll play games with you. *(He sings)*
    If memory serves, I still recall how
    When I was as young as you ladies are now
    When I'd finished with my classes
    And I'd finished with my chores
    Always there were taffy pulls and tug o' wars
    There were wienie roasts and treasure hunts
    Conundrums and charades
    Marching to Jerusalem and masquerades

    Oh, the singing and the dancing and the gaiety
    When I was a youthful member of the laity.

    So many ways to have good clean fun
    So many games to enjoy

No earthly reason why Jack should be
That dull, dull boy

Every so often we're overwhelmed
Too many things to be done
That's why it pays to have
So many ways to have
Good clean fun.

Now, isn't it rather a pity, my friends
That as we live our lives
We let our youthful pleasures slip away

ALL

Amen!

BROCK

We shouldn't forget how to kick up our heels
For many a time arrives
When levity is the order of the day

ALL

Like today!

BROCK

I'm in the mood for fun, my friends

ALL

Good clean fun

BROCK

Somebody name a game that we can play.

99

TENDERLOIN

GROUP

Let's play spoons
How about horns
No . . . clumps
Let's play goose
No, spoons . . . broom . . . horns . . . buzz . . . clumps
   . . . goose go bang
Six fans . . . authors . . . proverbs . . . parallels
Pebbles . . . magic . . . heads and bodies
Queen of Sheba . . . turn the trencher
Draw a pig . . . the wonderful tree
Cat and mouse . . . geographical game
Diamond ring . . . poetry making . . . musical chairs
   . . . wiggle waggle

Paddy from home . . . the parson's cat
Six penny telegrams . . . cards in a hat

Name the living statues
The memory game . . . suggestions
Blowing out the candle
Trades . . . and twenty questions

GIRLS

Here we go gathering nuts in May

ALL

With so many wonderful games to play
Nobody needs the Tenderloin.

ALL

Spoons, horns, clumps,
goose
Broom, buzz, go bang
Six fans, authors,
Proverbs, parallels
Pebbles, magic,
Heads and bodies,
Queen of Sheba
Turn the trencher
Draw a pig, the wonder-
ful tree
Cat and mouse, geo-
graphical game
Diamond ring, poetry
making
Musical chairs, wiggle
waggle
Paddy from home, the
parson's cat
Six penny telegrams,
cards in a hat

BROCK

So many ways to have
good clean fun
So many games to enjoy
No earthly reason why
Jack should be
That dull, dull boy

Every so often we're
overwhelmed
Too many things to be
done
That's why it pays to have

BROCK *and* GROUP

So many ways to have
Good clean fun.

(*They exit, singing*)

That's why it pays to have
So many ways to have
Good clean fun.

(*All are gone.* LAURA *and* TOMMY, *wearing riding clothes,
walk in at right, cautiously, looking about to see if they
are observed. They sit on a bench*)

TOMMY   Ellington asked me to have dinner with him, then later we can meet you and the Vandenbergs at the opera.

LAURA   I guess that's best. Uncle Fred is furious, Tommy.

TOMMY   Oh, that's what's the matter?

LAURA   He doesn't want me to see you any more.

TOMMY   Why?

LAURA   Well—

TOMMY   (*Sullen*)   'Cause I wasn't born rich, I suppose.
         (*He rises and crosses to left*)

LAURA   No. He thinks he knows how you're so prosperous. He says he knows where you get your money.
         (TOMMY *turns*)

TOMMY   (*Startled*)   He does? What's he say?

LAURA   He says you gamble.

TOMMY   (*Greatly relieved, sits on bench at left*)   Oh—Oh—(*It is growing dark*) (*Pretending contrite confession*) Well, it's true. (LAURA *crosses to him slowly. Facing her*) And I win—

LAURA   Don't you win at everything?

TOMMY   You know why? I got a lucky mascot. You know this picture you took of Dr. Brock? (*Takes out picture*) It brings me luck. I just put it down on the table, and you ought to see me draw cards!

(Offstage at right, voices sing "My Miss Mary." TOMMY
and LAURA *pause and look off at left)*

VOICES *(Off)*
My Miss Mary
Shy Miss Mary
Ever since we met, dear
I'm in fairyland
Would you be upset, dear
If I held your hand?
Shy Miss Mary
My Miss Mary
Time is passing by, Miss
Mary, don't be shy, Miss
Mary, won't you marry me?

LAURA He's threatened to cut off my income if I don't stop
seeing you, but I come of age next year. After all, I think I
should be able to select my own *friends. (Horses appear with
two girls on bridle path at left. A couple enters, crosses, and
exits at left.* LAURA *waves to the two girls)* There are the
others. There they are.

TOMMY *(Singing)*
I love you,

My Miss Mary
Shy Miss Mary

Ever since we met, dear
I'm in fairyland
Would you be upset, dear
If I held your hand?
(He kisses her)

Shy Miss Mary
My Miss Mary

Life could be so very
Extraordinary
Mary, won't you marry me?
I love you,
   (GROUP *enters upstage at left, and a couple comes in
   downstage at left.* GROUP *and* LAURA *sing*)

GROUP
   My Miss Mary
   Shy Miss Mary

LAURA
   Ever since we met, dear
   I'm in fairyland
   Would you be upset, dear
   If I held your hand?

LAURA *and* GROUP
   Shy Miss Mary
   My Miss Mary

TOMMY
   Life could be so very

LAURA
   Extraordinary

TOMMY
   Mary, won't you marry me?

GROUP

Marry me.

(TOMMY *and* LAURA *finish song at center.* WILLIE FRYE *appears at right, an ominous figure in the shadows*)

FRYE Tommy, you know where we can find Reverend Brock?

TOMMY (*Rising*) Why, yes, I think so. Sure.

FRYE Appreciate it.

TOMMY We're just going right by where he is.

FRYE Appreciate it.

(LAURA *and* TOMMY *go out at left.* SCHMIDT *appears at right and watches them*)

SCHMIDT That guy's making a pretty good thing of it, ain't he? Sometimes I wonder which side he's on. (*He crosses downstage. Horses go across the bridge from left to right. Voices are heard offstage at left.* SCHMIDT's *voice becomes sharp*) Here comes the preacher. Get out of here.

(FRYE *goes out at right.* BROCK *enters at left*)

SCHMIDT Your Reverence. (*No answer*) Sorry to interrupt you here, but something came up.

BROCK I think I can tell you what came up, Lieutenant Schmidt. (*Crosses to him*) The Governor has called a hearing to investigate the Tenderloin, and he has told the D.A. that if it isn't closed up tight, he'll be removed from office, and the D.A. has told you that if you don't clean it up, you'll be removed from office.

SCHMIDT   Right. And you done such good work in bringing this about, that some of your admirers got together and they want to reward you with a one-year trip to Europe—

BROCK *(Turning sharply)*   Silence! Don't sully your lips with bribes to me!
      (SCHMIDT *crosses hurriedly around* BROCK *and then speaks in front of him*)

SCHMIDT   Now wait a minute! You're a man of sense and I want to talk good plain sense to you. If there was a way to kill off whore houses—(BROCK *moves away;* SCHMIDT *follows*) —I'd do it as quick as you. Now them's rough words, but that's a fact. But we got to be practical. Shutting down the Tenderloin won't change a thing. If the houses close in my precinct, they'll only open again somewheres else.
      (BROCK *again moves away;* SCHMIDT *again follows*)

BROCK   That's an old argument, Lieutenant.

SCHMIDT   It's not an argument. It's facts. What do you think makes this the biggest city in the country? Why do out-of-towners come here? What keeps the bright lights burning and the green money circulating? Not your sermons, Your Reverence. It's sin. Sin is what makes this town go round. People want it. It's what keeps both you and me in business.

BROCK   Lieutenant Schmidt, you are an evil man.

SCHMIDT   I ain't no evil man. I got a little girl was just confirmed last week. (BROCK *crosses away;* SCHMIDT *follows*) No, sir. I'm just able to see facts.

BROCK   The facts are that this prostitution which you are trying to justify spreads disease and crime and degradation and
misery. It is an evil and I shall continue to fight it.

SCHMIDT   Mister—(BROCK *turns to him*)—I'm trying to give
you a chance to be a hero—take your winnings and go away.
But if you don't, then I'll skin you alive. I paid fifteen thou-
sand dollars to get transferred to this precinct. I mortgaged
my house to get that money. Now you want 'em to take my
house and disgrace me and my family!

BROCK   I am truly sorry for both you and your family—but
there is a penalty attached to sin.

SCHMIDT   There's a penalty attached to being too high and
mighty, too. I may lose my job, and you may lose your job—

BROCK   I very much doubt that, Lieutenant. You see, I work
for God.
    (BROCK *turns and strides out at left*)

SCHMIDT *(Shouting after him)*   All right, Holy Man, wait and
see!

Blackout

SCENE 2

A street.

A well-dressed man enters downstage at left. NELLIE *enters downstage at right and passes him.*

NELLIE (*Seductive*) Nice night . . . Ain't your name Eddie?

MAN No, Johnny.
    (SERGEANT *enters downstage at right.* NELLIE *sees him*)

NELLIE (*Sharp, to* MAN) Never mind. Beat it, beat it!
    (MAN *exits*)

SERGEANT (*Moving* NELLIE *off the stage*) Wasn't you told to keep off the streets? Now, off the streets! Want to get me in trouble? The Tenderloin is closed. Closed tight.
    (*They exit*)

Blackout

SCENE 3

Clark's.

GERTIE *is embroidering awkwardly at a table downstage.
Some of the other girls are lolling in the back.* FRYE *is seated
at stage right, studying a little black book, in which he makes
occasional notations.*

LIZ   Now, listen, ladies, I want you to quit your belly-aching.
We ain't closed down forever.
   (*Ad libs: "Sez you!" "I don't know about that," "Maybe
   we are."* NITA *enters during this. She walks down to*
   GERTIE)

NITA (*Taking embroidery*)   What you doin'?

GERTIE   Learning a trade.
   (NITA *examines* GERTIE'S *work*)

NITA   You'll starve.
   (*She crosses to a chair*)

GIRL   Damn that preacher.

MAGGIE (*Rises, crosses to* GIRL)   You know what we ought to
do? Make an image of him and stick pins in it.

GERTIE   It won't work. I tried it on my cousin once. Nothing.
(*Pricks her finger with the needle*) Ouch!

109

NITA (*Sits*) Why don't you quit that before you bleed to death?

LIZ (*At back*) You been askin' for a night off—now you got it.

GIRL I got a notion to get married.
(*All laugh*)

MAGGIE Hah!

GERTIE (*To* NITA) Hey, where's your ring?

NITA It's hid in a good safe place. I lost Joe, I ain't gonna lose the ring too.

GERTIE He may come back.

NITA It's got me buffaloed. He came in here every night, paying me twenty dollars just to talk to me—telling me how beautiful I am—then all of a sudden, he don't ever come back no more.

GERTIE Somebody else grabbed him off.

NITA I was getting real soft on that big fat slob. But I guess gents with coal mines don't go around loose forever.
(SCHMIDT *enters. All conversation stops.* FRYE *rises, moves to him*)

SCHMIDT You get Tommy?

FRYE He's coming.

SCHMIDT Coming? Why the hell ain't he here?

FRYE He's at the opera.

SCHMIDT The where?

FRYE The goddam opera. In a box. I tell him you want to see him. He says after the show. I tell him now, and then all those swells he's sitting with—they start shushing me until I had to get out.

SCHMIDT What about Deacon?

FRYE He's waiting in the back room.

SCHMIDT I want to talk to him.
(SCHMIDT *moves upstage and exits at right,* FRYE *following*)

GIRL I can get married any time I want to, to plenty of 'em.

GERTIE I could a got married last week.

NITA Who asked you?

GERTIE That cowboy.

NITA (*Disgusted*) He was drunk.

GERTIE (*Sighing*) Yeah, I know. That's why I gave him the gate. But one of these days some young Johnny will come along.

NITA You and your young Johnny. Quit dreamin'.

GERTIE That's all right. Just you watch—someday I'll get married.

NITA (*Indignant*) And work for nothin'? (*Rises, crosses slowly to right*) Not for me.

GERTIE (*Thoughtful*) I think I could get to like somebody, if he was permanent.

NITA Now you're getting sloppy. Don't be thinkin' about such things.

GERTIE (*Sighs*) I s'pose not . . .

NITA (*Sits and speaks softly, to herself*) Not for me. (*Then she sings*)
Oh, when will I find you
And where will we meet?
My gentle young Johnny
So steady and sweet
Oh, when will you come for me
When will you take me away?

You'll see what I am
And you'll know what I've done
And yet when you love me
You'll be the first one
My gentle young Johnny
Shall we be married today?

If you will be
My love, my own

You'll find a heart
No man has known
A heart
That's yours
Alone

If you will be tender
Then I shall be shy
From lower than low
I'll be higher than high
My gentle young Johnny
Shall we be married today?
    (JOE *enters*)

GERTIE (*To* NITA) Hey, psst . . .

NITA (*Sees* JOE) Well, you come back?

JOE Yeah. You busy?

NITA Ain't you heard?

JOE Oh, yeah. I forgot.

NITA Have a seat.
    (JOE *puts his hand into his pocket to take out money*)

NITA No. This is on the house. (JOE *sits facing her*) I ought
to pay you. You know why? 'Cause I missed you. (JOE *looks
down*) I thought maybe I wasn't never going to see you
again. Thought maybe you forgot all about me.

JOE (*Facing front*) I tried to.

NITA   That ain't very nice of you.

JOE   'Cause I been so unhappy.

NITA   I'm sorry. (*Touches him*) I don't want to make you unhappy, Joe.

JOE   I think I got to either see more of you or not at all. (*She
strokes his arm caressingly*) You wouldn't want to go away
some place with me, would you, Nita?

NITA   With you? (JOE *nods. She speaks dreamily*) I always
wanted to see China.

JOE   China?

NITA   Yeah, I used to have a Chinese gentleman call on me,
and he'd tell me all about Hong Kong and like that—

JOE   Well, you want to go see it?

NITA   Sure.

JOE   You do?

NITA   Why not? You're not pullin' my leg?

JOE   Oh, no.

NITA   All right, Joe, if you're sincere about it, then I will. Sure.
I'll go.

JOE   I'll treat you good. Honest, I will.

NITA But we got to plan it careful. (*Rises*) I don't want to get you in no trouble.

JOE What kind of trouble?

NITA With the law, you know. (*Sits on* JOE's *lap*) I guess we have to pretend like we're married, don't we?

JOE Gee, I don't know.

NITA Sure. A pal of mine—a Chicago girl—she told me. She and her gentleman got on so good that they really did get married.

JOE They did? (*She nods and snuggles to* JOE) Well, holy hen!
    (*He jumps up*)

NITA What's the matter, Joe?

JOE How about it? You want to get married?

NITA Ain't this kind of sudden?

JOE Well, it's practical, on account of the law. That's how I come to think of it.

NITA (*Nodding*) You're the boss, Joe. Whatever you say.

JOE (*Yells*) Yow!!

GERTIE (*Startled*) What's the matter?
    (NITA *crosses to* GERTIE)

JOE We're going to get married!
   (*Music starts*)

GERTIE (*To others*) Did you hear that, girls?
   (GERTIE *and* NITA *embrace. The other girls chatter*)

GIRL Married? To him?

LIZ On the level?

GIRL Ain't that swell?

GERTIE And he looks happy, too.
   (*They sing a reprise version of "The Picture of Happiness"*)

GIRLS

There are roses in his cheeks now
People listen when he speaks now
   (JOE *crosses toward left*)
No one like him
Since he landed Salome!

From a simple beginning
Just see how his sinning has paid
He's the picture of heavenly happiness
Now that he's made—
The grade!
   (JOE *exits at left. The girls gather around* NITA, *congratulating her and cheering.* TOMMY *enters in well-fitting white tie and tails*)

LIZ (*Seeing him*) Tommy, wait here!
   (LIZ *goes out upstage*)

GERTIE Tommy, what do you think! (*Crosses to* TOMMY) Nita's going to marry the fat guy!

NITA (*Haughty, crosses away*) You're gettin' things kind of mixed up, Gertie. Nita ain't marrying a fat guy; she's marryin' a heavy-set millionaire!

TOMMY (*Crosses to* NITA) Well, congratulations.

NITA (*Sarcastic*) Yeah, I been improving my mind: I found out something—diamonds come from coal.
> (NITA *and* GERTIE *cross and exit upstage at left.* FRYE, SCHMIDT, *and* DEACON *enter at rear.* FRYE *and* DEACON *remain upstage*)

SCHMIDT (*Crosses to* TOMMY) Thanks for coming.

TOMMY I got here as fast as I could. I didn't like to bust away in the middle of the opera. (*Short laugh*) I had some explaining to do as it was 'cause they were all going to Delmonico's. I told them I'd most likely join them there later.

SCHMIDT (*Dry*) You must do that.

TOMMY (*Looking from one to the other*) Did you want to ask me something?

SCHMIDT (*Innocent*) How's everything over at the church?

TOMMY (*Hasty*) I tried finding some dirt about the Reverend, like you told me, but nobody knows anything.

SCHMIDT (*Slow*) I hear you got a photograph of the Preacher that brings you luck.

TOMMY Oh, yeah. (*Laughs*) Won again last night—didn't I, Deacon? Ninety-six bucks.

SCHMIDT Let's have a look at it.

TOMMY Huh? The picture? (*Takes out picture*) Oh, it's nothing.
(*He holds the picture toward* SCHMIDT, *who takes* TOMMY's *hand to steady it and looks at the picture. Then* SCHMIDT *takes it, and looks at it more closely*)

SCHMIDT Not bad. (*Calling*) Deacon.
(DEACON *comes over and takes the picture*)

DEACON (*Nodding*) Sure.

SCHMIDT Can you do it?

DEACON It'll come out fine.
(*He passes the picture to* SCHMIDT)

SCHMIDT Leave me keep this a couple of days, will you, Tommy?

TOMMY Why? What do you want it for?

SCHMIDT (*Tough*) You're on our side, ain't you?

TOMMY Sure, I am.

SCHMIDT (*To* DEACON) You want one of the girls from here?

DEACON Yes—and I'll need a bed, too.

118

SCHMIDT (*Sardonic*) A bed. Now, where can we find a bed around here?

TOMMY (*As* SCHMIDT *laughs at his own joke*) Wait a minute, now. That picture is a personal thing. (SCHMIDT *looks up*) I don't know what you want it for, but—

SCHMIDT (*Hard*) You're damn right it's personal. Kid—(*Slaps* TOMMY *on the back*)—you just earned your percentage. Now get the hell out of here.

TOMMY What are you going to do?

SCHMIDT (*Walking him to rear*) It's none of your business what I'm gonna do. (*Pause*) Now get out! (TOMMY *exits rapidly at right*) And turn left for Delmonico's!

Blackout

SCENE 4

The trial.

JESSICA *and* LAURA *appear in front of scrim depicting* Tatler *newspaper. They read the paper.*

JESSICA (*Singing*)
>See, Laura, what it says here
>Here in this wicked paper

LAURA
>Oh, what a dreadful scandal!

LAURA *and* JESSICA
>Reverend Brock takes the stand
>Reverend Brock spills the dirt
>   (PURDY *and* JOE *enter at left carrying copies of the* Tatler)

PURDY
>Joe, have you seen this paper?
>Our church in such a scandal
>It's utterly disgraceful!

PURDY *and* JOE
>Reverend Brock takes the stand
>Reverend Brock spills the dirt

120

Reverend Brock testifies
> (*Upstage we now see stylized trial through scrim. Figures mouth testimony as characters read from their newspapers downstage*)

LAURA (*As* BROCK *mouths*)
> These girls who ply their illegal wares
> Must first make sure the police get theirs

JOE *and* PURDY (*As the* CHAIRMAN *pantomimes upstage*)
> Did you witness violations?

LAURA *and* JESSICA (*As* BROCK *pantomimes*)
> We did!

JOE *and* PURDY
> Did you take down conversations?

LAURA *and* JESSICA
> We did!

JOE *and* PURDY
> Do we understand that you yourselves
> Received solicitations, God forbid?

LAURA *and* JESSICA
> We did!
> (*As the prostitutes pantomime upstage*)

> So many ways to have good clean fun!

PURDY (*Speaking*)   Come on in, honey, be a sport.

MEN (*Upstage*)
> All night, time and again we saw

LAURA *and* JESSICA
> So many games to enjoy

PURDY (*Speaking*) Got a double eagle?

MEN
> Girls who break every moral law

LAURA *and* JESSICA
> See why it pays to have
> So many ways to have
> Good clean fun!

PURDY (*Speaking*) We're open on Sundays!

ALL
> Then the Lieutenant, the well-known Pantata
> Spoke up in a voice unexpectedly calm
> Coldly ignoring the minister's charges
> He sprang to his feet . . .

LAURA
> Continued on page four . . .
>> (*She pauses to turn page*)
> And ignited a bomb!

JESSICA (*As the Pantata pantomimes*)
> Reverend Brock who's been acting so holy
> This Reverend Brock who the city admires
> Why do you think he went down to the Tenderloin?
> Just to indulge his immoral desires!

ALL (*Upstage as the chorus pantomimes shock*)
No! No!
This is impossible!
No! No!
This cannot be!
No! No!
Not such a man as he!

JESSICA
I got the proof here
This picture was took
On the night that the Preacher was
Out fightin' sin
I'm gonna show you a copy made big
So you'll see how this minister took you all in.
Look, look, this is your minister!
   (*Above the* CHAIRMAN *appears a large blowup of a snap-shot showing* REVEREND BROCK *in bed with a naked girl*)

ALL (*Horrified*)
Look!
Look!
That's Doctor Brock!

Look! Look!
What an incredible shock!
See the headline
The preacher's a lecher
Disaster demolishes pastor's campaign!

Blackout

SCENE 5

The lights come up on a celebration at Clark's.

Boys and girls are dancing together, and then FRYE—*dressed as a burlesqued imitation of* BROCK—*and* GERTIE *are carried in.* FRYE *is placed on a table at center.*

LIZ Here he is, ladies and gents, the Reverend Dr. Brock!
    (*The crowd jeers*)

FRYE (*Falsetto*) Do you know what you are?

GIRLS Whaaaat?

FRYE (*Pompous*) Monuments to harlotry—(*Crowd laughs*)
  And I'm here to find out why! (FRYE *sings*)
    I've come down here you understand
    Only to collect information
    All I want is figures and facts

GROUP
    Just figures and facts

FRYE
    For my education.

ALL
    Old Doc Brock went out on the town
    Trying to collect information

124

All that work got Brock overheated
So he completed his education.
   (*They dance*)

FRYE

   Look at all the evidence
   What a lot of evidence
   Goodness, this is fun
   And I've just begun
   To scratch the surface
   Oh, for pity's sake what did I say?

GIRLS

   Here's a piece of evidence
   Here's a piece
   Here's a piece
   Here's a piece of evidence,
   Take it like a man!
      (*The dance builds to orgiastic proportions*)

Blackout

SCENE 6

Parish House. Night.

BROCK *is alone on the stage, seated, reading the Bible.*

BROCK (*He hears a sound. He turns, startled, and rises*) Who?

TOMMY (*Entering*) It's me. I've just come from Clark's and I wanted to see you.

BROCK I left word that I was not to be disturbed, but I'm glad you came, Tom. I'm glad you're here.

TOMMY I came because I wanted you to know—(*He hesitates*) —to know that I'm sorry. About what happened.

BROCK Thank you. (BROCK *picks up the Bible and sits down.* TOMMY *crosses and sits beside him*) They jeered at me, Tom. As I left the hearing, people jeered at me.

TOMMY Damn 'em!

BROCK (*Steadier now*) At first, I could scarcely understand. I could not grasp what had happened to me. But then, gradually, as the truth came home, I wanted to run. Like a schoolboy. Run and hide. I came here to hide myself.

TOMMY Dr. Brock, you should have got up and said something. You should have denied it.

126

BROCK I was numb, I couldn't think. Lieutenant Schmidt said he'd skin me alive, and he did.

TOMMY When they call you back tomorrow, you've got to deny it. They'll believe you. Dr. Brock, you're the best man that ever lived.

BROCK No, I'm not. But I thank you for your faith in me. I'm glad to know that you're still my friend.

TOMMY Oh, God. (*Savage*) I ain't prayin', I'm cussin'! I'm cussin' the injustice of things. Like that picture.

BROCK I know that the picture is false, Tom, that it was made up of bits and pieces. I know it, and Schmidt knows it.

TOMMY It was a lousy thing to do.

BROCK Yes, it was . . . contemptible, but people will do many things for money.

TOMMY People are rotten.

BROCK No, Tom, people are good, fundamentally good. You must believe that.

TOMMY No, I don't believe it. I don't believe in anything. People are rotten, everyone of us. We're all rotten. It isn't fair. A person wants to get somewheres, he wants to get something out of life . . . It just ain't fair.
(TOMMY *rushes out;* BROCK *looks worriedly after him*)

Blackout

SCENE 7

Precinct street.

A line of people await BROCK.

MRS. BARKER Here comes Dr. Brock now.
    (BROCK *enters*)

NELLIE (*Contemptuous*) That's him! That's the dirty preacher!

MAN (*Snarls*) Damn hypocrite!

WOMAN (*Vicious*) I hope they give it to him good!

ANOTHER WOMAN You're a disgrace!
    (*The scrim rises.* BROCK *goes to the witness chair. The crowd drifts into place*)

SCENE 8

The courtroom.

This scene is played realistically.

CHAIRMAN Dr. Brock, have you anything to say about the picture? How do you explain the picture?

SCHMIDT He can't. Because there's no way of explaining the picture. It's there. Everybody seen it. It's the truth and he can't explain away the truth.
(*The crowd reacts*)

CHAIRMAN Order!

SCHMIDT It proves he's a liar, a fraud, a lecher . . . a dirty old man!
(*The crowd reacts*)

LAURA Jessica, I can't stand it!

TOMMY (*Stands up in rear of crowd*) Wait! (*Silence*) The picture's a fake!

SCHMIDT (*Roars*) Sit down, you!

TOMMY (*Crossing downstage*) No, I won't! It's a fake!

SCHMIDT Throw him out of here!

TOMMY Not 'til you see this. I got the negative. I got the negative right here. The picture they used to make that thing. It was taken with my camera down at the beach. Schmidt made me give it to him. He rigged it. He rigged it to fix Dr. Brock.

SCHMIDT I'll get you! (SCHMIDT *grapples with* TOMMY, *who squirms free.* SCHMIDT *turns to the* COMMISSIONERS *on the bench*) Are you going to take evidence from that rat? He ain't to be trusted. He takes a percentage off houses of prostitution! His best friends is street women!

LAURA No!

SCHMIDT He's a crook!

LAURA It's not true!

TOMMY (*Desperate*) Yes, it is. It's true. It's all true . . . but not the way it sounds. Please . . .

BROCK Tom!
        (LAURA *runs out.* PURDY *stops* TOMMY *from following*)

SCHMIDT (*To* SERGEANT) Get him! And get him hard!

CHAIRMAN Come back here! Order! Order! (*The crowd subsides*) Dr. Brock, I believe this commission owes you an apology.

BROCK Sir, this commission has done its duty.

SCHMIDT (*Furious*) I ain't finished yet!

BROCK Lieutenant Schmidt, this last act of yours will assuredly
close the Tenderloin.
        (*The crowd cheers*)

The Lights Dim Out

SCENE 9

A street.

SCHMIDT *is waiting;* FRYE *enters.*

SCHMIDT Well?

FRYE Everything quiet.

SCHMIDT Quiet as a grave, eh, Willie?

FRYE Yeah. You can walk the length of Twenty-third Street and not see a light. Shutters on the windows—no music, no nothing.

SCHMIDT *(Sadly)* Goddam it, every time I think of it, it gives me indigestion.

FRYE Clark's is dead. They got a padlock on the door. All the girls are going west.

SCHMIDT Somebody's gonna pay for this. Didn't you find that rat-faced Howatt guy for me?

FRYE Not yet, but I got the Gallagher boys layin' for him, Lieutenant. They'll find him.

SCHMIDT They damn well better.

132

FRYE Right, Lieutenant.

SCHMIDT I may not be Lieutenant for long, so get used to calling me something else.

FRYE Very good, Sergeant.

SCHMIDT (*Reacts*) Huh? Could be.

MARGIE'S VOICE (*Offstage at left*) Come on, girls, we'll be late.

FRYE (*Pointing offstage left*) Will ya look what's comin'!

SCHMIDT I can't stand it. It's startin' up my gas pains again. Come on, let's get out of here.
> (SCHMIDT *and* FRYE *exit at right; the girls enter at left. They carry suitcases and personal possessions that indicate they are leaving town*)

LIZ (*Singing*)
Little Old New Yo

MARGIE
Ho-ho-ho-hork

ALL
Little Old New Yo ho ho ho ho hork
Every other girl has four problems
Four problems a year
Not five like we got here

FIRST GIRL
Shelter

NELLIE
> Food

SECOND GIRL
> Clothing

THIRD GIRL
> Men

GIRLS
> And reform!
> Reform, reform
> It's gotten a bit too warm
> I never thought I'd live to see the day
> Reform would come to stay.

LIZ
> Don't lose your faith in human nature
> We may still be saved

MARGIE
> There is comfort in the fact
> Men are basically depraved

GIRLS
> Little Old New Yo ho ho ho ho hork
> Little Old New Yo ho ho ho ho hork
> Little Old New Yo ho ho ho ho hork.

Blackout

SCENE 10

Parish House.

LAURA *and* JESSICA *enter at left, carrying a rack full of letters which they are opening and sorting.* JOE *is standing to one side in a new suit.* BROCK *walks back and forth.*

JESSICA This is a personal—
      (*She passes the letter to* LAURA, *who gives it to* BROCK)

LAURA So many people who are happy for you, Dr. Brock.

BROCK (*Standing next to* LAURA) My dear children—I'll confess that this vindication—well, the relief is almost more than I can bear.

LAURA Your true friends never doubted you.

BROCK Not my true friends.

JOE Dr. Brock, do you consider Tommy Howatt a true friend?

BROCK Of course I do.

JOE I'd like to have him come to the wedding, if you've got no objections.

BROCK Do you know where he is?

135

JOE   He's hid out where the Pantata's gang can't find him. But Nita knew where to send him a message, so she did.

BROCK   Capital! I want to see him.

JESSICA   Well, come on, Laura—to work—to work—to work—
        (*They go out upstage at left*)

JOE   Reverend Brock, I ain't very good at saying thanks, but this marryin' Nita and I, it just shows how broad-minded you are and all.

BROCK   Now, Joe, it isn't that I approve of what you're doing.

JOE   Oh, I don't approve of it, either, but I want to do it. And this is once nothin' can stop me.

BROCK   I am sure the young lady has many fine characteristics.

JOE   Wait'll you meet her. Reverend Brook, she's so beautiful. She's like an angel—
        (PURDY *enters at left. His manner is brusque*)

PURDY   Dr. Brock, may I speak to you?

BROCK   Come in, my friend.

JOE   I'll wait for you out there.
        (*He goes out upstage at left*)

PURDY   Dr. Brock, I may as well get on with this—get it over.

BROCK   The Elders have adjourned?

PURDY They have. They've delegated me.

BROCK Yes?

PURDY Dr. Brock, your campaign against the Tenderloin has been a success. It is closed up, at least for the time being, and your personal conduct has been vindicated. The Board appreciates your zeal.

BROCK I could have done no less.

PURDY But some feel that the serenity of our church has been destroyed. (*Crosses in front of* BROCK) Dr. Brock, we wish to get back the church we had before you created all this agitation. (BROCK *looks at him—very still*) We know you have had many calls from other congregations. And so—painful as it is, we feel that it might be best for all to have you make a change at this time. (*They look at each other;* BROCK *is stunned*) Regretfully, we ask for your resignation.

(JESSICA *enters upstage at left*)

JESSICA Pardon me.

PURDY (*Annoyed*) Yes?

JESSICA Dr. Brock, Mr. Kovack's financée has arrived, and he wondered should he bring her in?

BROCK (*Turns slowly. Dully*) I'd be happy to meet her.
(JESSICA *exits*)

PURDY (*Puzzled*) Fiancée? Joe?

137

BROCK (*He looks up*) How did you vote?

PURDY I thought you should go.

BROCK (*Slow*) Perhaps I should.
    (JESSICA *enters and crosses downstage at left*)

JESSICA I'll show you the way.
    (PURDY *crosses to the right.* NITA, *in a tasteful new suit, comes in with* JOE *upstage at left*)

JOE Reverend Brock, may I have the honor to present Miss Nita Merini.

BROCK Come in, my dear, and welcome.
    (NITA *shyly crosses* JOE *and shakes hands, then retreats back to* JOE. PURDY *crosses upstage right, stops, and stares with disapproval*)

JOE She's been buying clothes all the afternoon.

BROCK (*Polite*) That's a very becoming outfit.

NITA (*Anxious*) It's all right, then? I mean, for the ceremony? It's the right thing?

BROCK (*Smiles*) It's charming.

JOE (*To* NITA) See, I told you—

NITA Joe—Mr. Kovack—he thinks everything is going to work out all right.

138

BROCK   We all hope so.

JOE   It'll be my fault if it don't.

NITA   (*Fierce*)   No, it'll be my fault. 'Cause he's a good man. And I'm going to try.

BROCK   I'm sure you are.
   (JOE *takes* NITA's *hand and starts leading her off to left. She stops and turns*)

NITA   (*Halting, awkward*)   When I went to the store today, I took off everything I had on. And I says, throw it away, put on everything new. Just for the idea of it, you know. Excuse me.
   (*She goes out with* JESSICA, *who takes her hand*)

PURDY   (*Indignant*)   Joe, don't tell me you're planning to marry this girl!

JOE   (*Grim*)   Mr. Purdy—

PURDY   (*Irritable*)   Speak up. What is it?

JOE   (*Cold*)   You ain't invited!   (PURDY *exits in a huff at right.* JOE *crosses to right, shaking his fist, speaking to* BROCK)   If you hadn't been here, I'd have given him a punch in the nose.
   (LAURA *enters upstage at left*)

LAURA   Tommy Howatt's coming! I saw him out the window!

BROCK (*Crossing into office*) Good. Make him welcome. I'll be back. Come with me, Joe.

(BROCK *exits into the office, followed by* JOE. TOMMY *enters, carrying a bundle of clothes tied to his cane*)

LAURA Come in.

TOMMY I didn't know I was going to see you. I was coming to the wedding, but I can't even wait for that now 'cause they're after me. Do you hate me?

LAURA No. Are you all right?

TOMMY Sure. I'm just on the run. But I'm all right. I got me a job in Denver. I'm going west.

LAURA (*Singing softly*)
Tommy, Tommy,
How I'll miss you
More than I can say.

TOMMY
Laura, I'll miss you.

LAURA
Tommy, I'm so proud
To know you
Proud to know the boy
Who let the nice young man
Come through.

TOMMY I tell you what. I'll come back east some day. And I'll look you up. Ring your doorbell. Bridget'll say, "Well, if it isn't Mr. Thomas Dubonnet Howatt, the Third." "No," I'll say, "just plain Tom Howatt, the fellow who owns all those gold mines and he's come back to . . ." (*Pause*) So just don't forget me.

LAURA (*Low, tearful*) Good-bye, Tommy Howatt.
(*She exits.* BROCK *enters*)

BROCK Well, Thomas. I see you're dressed for traveling.

TOMMY They got clean air in Denver, I hear. I came to give the bride away. But I spotted a couple a thugs following me, so you'll forgive me if I sneak out the back door.

BROCK Soon I'll be leaving, too. I hear the air in Detroit is also highly recommended.

TOMMY (*Shocked*) They kicked you out? After all you did?

BROCK (*Smiles*) After all *we* did. You share the credit. In fact, I have been thinking of making you the subject of my initial sermon.

TOMMY (*Laughs*) Yeah. "How to Go to Hell in One Easy Lesson."

BROCK Not Hell. If anything, you've moved in the opposite direction.

TOMMY You wouldn't ever be in Denver, would you?

BROCK Who can say? I never thought I'd be in Detroit.

TOMMY I was up half the night, trying to think of something I had, some present to give you.

BROCK You've given me one already, Tom. You've given me back my name.

TOMMY I got nothing for you, Dr. Brock. Nothing but me.

BROCK (*Choked up*) That's a rich gift. Good-bye, Tom.
(*They shake hands*)

TOMMY So long. I wish I could be there for that sermon.

BROCK It might embarrass you. It's full of admiration and gratitude.

TOMMY Go easy—don't make me out a saint.
(TOMMY *exits*)

BROCK (*Gentle laugh*) A saint? Hardly. No power on earth could do that.

Blackout

BROCK *is on the pulpit. Music is heard in the background.*

BROCK   Nor, good people of Detroit, could any earthly power have made this young man sacrifice the things he did. To save a friend he was willing to risk everything he held most dear—money, position, even the girl he loved. Everywhere we look, we find good intermixed with evil. But if we wish the good to triumph, we must fight for it. And here in Detroit, there is a condition which I cannot overlook. For there is a district from Maple Street to the waterfront that is a veritable Sodom and Gomorrah.

> (*The lights come up on motionless figures in Limbo. They are silent as* BROCK *continues to address his new congregation, and then they begin to move and dance and sing "Little Old Detroit." These characters are no different from the ones in the Tenderloin*)

GIRLS
Little Old Detroit
Is plenty good enough for me
Good enough for me
Good enough for me
Little Old Detroit
Is plenty good enough for me
Keep your hands off
Little Old Detroit.

BROCK (*Speaking*)   I ask each and every one of you to join me in a great crusade. Let us put on the shield and buckler of righteousness. Let us grasp the two-edged sword of faith and duty. Let us go forth fearlessly to uproot this evil, to drive this scourge from our midst. Let us fight the good fight.

Little Old Detroit
Is plenty good enough for
me
Big enough for me
Rich enough for me

ALL

Little Old Detroit
Is plenty good enough for
me
Tell your friends to
Keep their hands off
Little . . .
Old . . .
Detroit!
(*Their singing drowns* BROCK *out*)

(BROCK *continues speaking but cannot be heard as the music builds*) "The first angel sounded his trumpet and there followed hail mingled with blood; and the third part of the trees was burned up and the green grass and the great mountains burning like fire was cast into the sea . . ."

Curtain